Horribly ★ FAMOUS

CHARLES DICKENS
and his Pen Pals

by Tracey Turner

Illustrated by Goddard

000000
D1354013

Scholastic Children's Books,
Euston House, 24 Eversholt Street,
London NW1 1DB, UK

A division of Scholastic Ltd
London ~ New York ~ Toronto ~ Sydney ~ Auckland
Mexico City ~ New Delhi ~ Hong Kong

First published in the UK by Scholastic Ltd, 2005
This edition published 2012

Text © Tracey Turner, 2005, 2012
Illustrations © Clive Goddard, 2005
Cover illustration © Dave Smith, 2012

All rights reserved

ISBN 978 1407 12409 4

Page layout services provided by Quadrum Solutions Ltd, Mumbai, India
Printed and bound by CPI Group (UK) Ltd, Croydon, CR0 4YY

2 4 6 8 10 9 7 5 3 1

The right of Tracey Turner and Clive Goddard to be identified as the
author and illustrator respectively of this work has been asserted by them
in accordance with the Copyright, Designs and Patents Act, 1988.

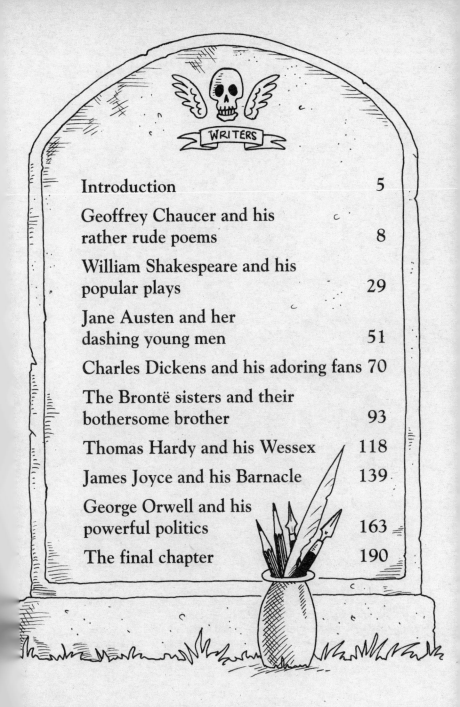

WRITERS

INTRODUCTION

Charles Dickens is two hundred years old and, just like the other people in this book, he's still famous. He didn't change the world by conquering an empire, or exploring Antarctica, or inventing the light bulb – he changed it by writing things down.

You can probably think of loads of horribly famous writers…

We couldn't squeeze all of them into this book, otherwise it would have been the size of Grimsby, but the ten writers you'll meet here are some of the most famous ever.

Writers are, of course, famous for … writing. But that doesn't mean they didn't do some surprising things as well. For example, did you know…

• Charles Dickens was a child labourer in a shoe-polish factory?

• Emily Brontë put out her brother when he caught fire?

• Thomas Hardy worked in a graveyard?

• William Shakespeare was put on trial by Elizabeth I?

• James Joyce wanted to open a fireworks factory?

And that's just in real life. In their writing anything can happen: ghosts, murders, magic, passionate lurve and terrible revenge.

Read on and find out about the famous writers who created some of the most gripping plots and memorable characters ever – words that are wonderful enough to stand the test of time and still make people laugh and cry today. Take a peek at some incredibly revealing secret diaries, discover what was going on in the Victorian celebrity magazine *Good Day!*, and see if you can work out what inspired these writers to create stories that have changed lives.

After all, as someone once said…

The pen is mightier than the sword.

… and a lot easier to write with.

GEOFFREY CHAUCER AND HIS RATHER RUDE POEMS

Geoffrey Chaucer is *still* horribly famous, as 'the father of English poetry', more than 600 years after he died. Even though the world has changed massively in that 600 years – so much that Geoffrey would probably struggle to recognize it as the same planet – people are still reading the words he wrote. Some of which are really rather rude.

We know a lot about some of the famous writers in this book. But Geoffrey lived during the Middle Ages – such a long time ago that we don't know all that much. Not even his birthday...

Meet the Chaucers

Geoffrey was born in London to parents who were rich and well-connected. But no one knows the exact date, which will be a big disappointment to you if you were thinking of throwing a birthday party for him. We don't even know the year – the best we can do is say it was some time between 1340 and 1343. It'd be nice if we could tell you about Geoffrey's brothers and sisters ... but sadly we can't.

We do know that Geoffrey's dad was a wine merchant and that the family lived in a big house in an area of London called Vintry ('vintner' is another name for a wine merchant).

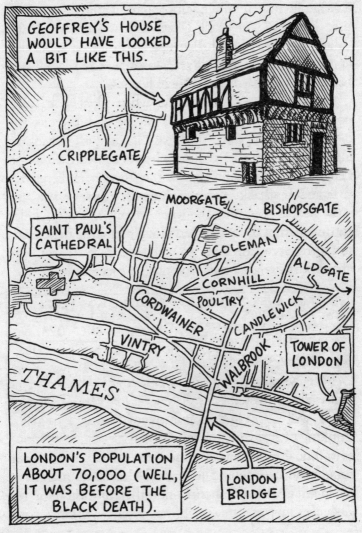

The bothersome Black Death

In 1347 Geoffrey's father was called away to Southampton on business and the family went with him. While they were away from London, the whole country was struck by a rather inconvenient and unpleasant feature of medieval life: the plague, or Black Death as it was known. It was called the *Black* Death because of the black spots that appeared on victims' skin. It was called the Black *Death* because … well, you can probably guess.

London was just about the worst place you could possibly be during a spot of plague because the city was overcrowded and dirty, so disease spread fast. It was also full of rats, whose fleas bit people and caused the disease. People at the time didn't realize this, though, and preferred to blame the Black Death on things like cats, 'bad air' and nasty people poisoning the water supply. 'Cures' included cutting victims to let out 'bad blood', drinking treacle and strapping live chickens to plague sores. As you can imagine, they didn't have a very high success rate.

In fact, the Black Death managed to kill a third of the population of England and maybe as many as half of the people who lived in London. If it wasn't for Mr Chaucer's job, Geoffrey might never have written a word.

School, and a new page

The Chaucers returned to London in 1350, after the plague outbreak was over, and young Geoffrey was probably sent to one of the schools near his home: rich kids were usually sent to school around the age of seven. Here's what he would have been taught:

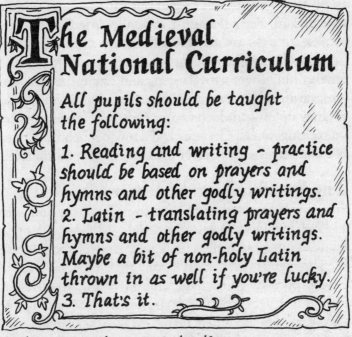

The Medieval National Curriculum

All pupils should be taught the following:

1. Reading and writing - practice should be based on prayers and hymns and other godly writings.
2. Latin - translating prayers and hymns and other godly writings. Maybe a bit of non-holy Latin thrown in as well if you're lucky.
3. That's it.

And you moan about your school?

Geoffrey was probably taught his thrilling subjects in French. From 1066, when the Norman William the Conqueror became king, England had been run by French nobles, so French was the language of posh people and especially the royal court. (Although gradually they took to speaking English like everyone else.) During Geoffrey's lifetime things were changing – not surprising when you think that this was nearly 300 years after the Norman Conquest. By the end of his life schools were teaching children in English, and not many English people were fluent in French.

In 1357 young Geoffrey (he was between 14 and 17) was sent off to be a page in a VIP household – none other than that of Prince Lionel (well, you can't have everything), King Edward III's son. A page's job was a sort of cross between a job and an education: he was a household servant, waiting on the family at meals and entertaining them with dancing and singing, but he was also taught subjects such as languages, grammar and how to draw up official documents. Although it sounds a bit unexciting, in fact Geoffrey had a top job: he would have been among the most privileged young men of his age.

The horrible Hundred Years War

France and England had been at war for some time – in 1337, King Edward III (then only 18) laid claim to France's throne as well as England's. Understandably, the French were rather upset about this, especially since Edward already ruled large chunks of the area that is France today. So the two countries went to war ... for 116 years! The Hundred Years War (as it became known afterwards – not during, for obvious reasons) continued, with a few intermissions, tea-breaks, etc, until 1453, when English King Henry VI finally gave up his claim to the French throne.

But in Geoffrey's day the War was still raging away. Continuing a typical medieval career path, Geoffrey joined the army in 1359 as a squire (a sort of knight's assistant) and was sent off to France to fight.

The secret diary of Geoffrey Chaucer, *
aged (roughly) 18½

I thought going to war would be glamorous and exciting. I didn't think I'd end up in a dark, damp dungeon counting the hours until (if??) I can get back home. But here I am.

I was only too happy to go off to fight for King Edward against those good-for-nothing French types (who do they think they are, refusing to be ruled by our glorious King??). I was looking forward to my first real battle, the clash of fine English swords and the whistle of the arrows as the cowardly Frenchies begged us for mercy. In fact I was even secretly hoping that more knights might be needed and that someone would club me 'Sir Geoffrey' on the battlefield due to my fearlessness in the face of death.

But when it came to it, it wasn't like that at all. We didn't do any charging into

* Translated from the original Middle English – more on that later.

battle. There was a group of us creeping about in the dark one night, in a place called Rethel, near Reims. We were looking for food and supplies. It was pouring with rain, freezing cold and I was thinking things couldn't get much worse, when all of a sudden they did: I was collared by a burly great Frenchman.

That's how I've ended up here, in prison, with the other knights and squires, waiting until someone pays for us all to be released and sent back to England. I hope they hurry up - the damp's making my armour go rusty. Maybe there's a less risky profession I could try.

Geoffrey had to wait four long months before he was ransomed (money was paid to the French in return for his release). He was finally ransomed for £16 – the same amount as the ransom of one of the war horses! Maybe the experience put him off the army for life, because he never went to war again.

Geoffrey and Philippa

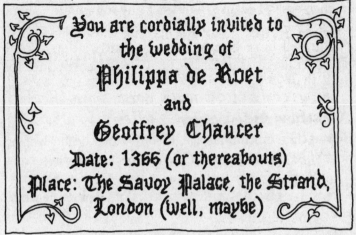

You are cordially invited to
the wedding of
Philippa de Roet
and
Geoffrey Chaucer
Date: 1366 (or thereabouts)
**Place: The Savoy Palace, the Strand,
London (well, maybe)**

By 1366 Geoffrey was married to Philippa de Roet, a lady-in-waiting to the Queen, which was a very important job to have.

It was quite common at the time to marry for increased status or wealth (it still is, but in the Middle Ages it wasn't seen as a bad thing to do). Since Geoffrey and Philippa both had top jobs in the royal household and seem to have spent as much time as possible apart, maybe they got married just for that reason. For many years Philippa lived in Lincolnshire with John of Gaunt's family (who owned the Savoy Palace in the Strand – we'll find out about him later), while Geoffrey lived in London.

Geoffrey and Philippa did have children together. One of them was a daughter, Elizabeth, who became a nun in 1381. Thomas Chaucer was born in 1367 and ended up with a royal job like his dad – in fact, Thomas became rich and successful and *his* daughter ended up as the Duchess of Suffolk (now *there's* posh). Geoffrey also had a son called Lewis, for whom he wrote a kind of children's science book. Because there isn't any information about Lewis as an adult, it's likely that he died young. There might well have been other kids that we don't know about. Philippa died in 1387, so the pair were married for more than 20 years.

A rather rude poem

By the time of his marriage, Geoffrey had begun writing poetry. At first he wrote in French, because it was seen as the only proper poetical language (since it was spoken by toffs and not by the common herd). But Geoffrey began to write his poetry in English – and he started a fashion for it (which is why he's called 'the father of English poetry'). One of the first things he wrote was a translation of a well-known French poem, the highly raunchy *Romance of the Rose*. Here are a few (non-raunchy) lines from it:

> *Though we mermaydens clepe hem here*
> *In English, as is oure usaunce,*
> *Men clepe hem sereyns in Fraunce.*

Straight away you'll notice something: yes, Chaucer was absolutely rubbish at spelling. Not really. The reason Geoffrey's words look a bit weird is that he and everyone else 600 years ago spoke English, but not as we know it. We now call it Middle English. Translated into modern English, the above lines mean:

> *Though we call them mermaids here*
> *In English, as is our custom,*
> *Men call them sirens in France.*

Not all that different, really. As you'll know if you've had a conversation with your granny recently, language changes from generation to generation. Over centuries it can change massively. It might well be that, in 600 years' time, someone reading your English homework won't have a clue what you were on about.

Geoffrey went on to write his own poems as well as translating other people's, as we'll find out. But he did have other things to occupy his time…

Top jobs

Medieval Royal Diplomat Wanted

To carry out Top Secret Missions on the King's Business

Applications are invited from candidates with training as a page (preferably in a royal household like Prince Lionel's) and several years' experience of the Royal Court. The following are essential for all applicants:

• Absolute loyalty to the King of England
• Excellent diplomatic skills, even when faced with murderous Italian tyrants
• Excellent secret-keeping skills

In return, we offer foreign travel, a competitive salary and gifts for life from His Royal Majesty (if he thinks you deserve it).

That's the job Geoffrey ended up getting – in the service of King Edward III. His job meant that he travelled around Europe a fair bit. When you think that there were no cars, trains or planes, this was quite an achievement. As early as 1366, when Geoffrey was about 24, he was sent by King Edward to Spain, probably on a secret mission. Unfortunately, it was so secret that we don't know what he was up to … but it would be nice to think of Geoffrey as a sort of medieval James Bond.

The King also sent him to Italy twice, probably to meet the banking families who held the King's debts in Florence (where the biggest banks in Europe were). On his second visit in 1372 Geoffrey stayed for five months, and might have met up with the famous Italian poet Petrarch while he was there.

There were other opportunities for foreign travel, too. Some of them probably involved scouring Europe for a suitable wife for the King who came after Edward, Richard II. The scariest trip of all must have been the one to Lombardy in Italy in 1378…

The secret diary of Geoffrey Chaucer, aged (roughly) 27½

Now that I've finally arrived in Lombardy after weeks of bumpy rides and sick-making sea voyages I'm beginning to wish I'd stayed at home. I've been sent to meet the Visconti brothers, the rulers here, and ask if one of their daughters fancies being Queen of England – a rather delicate matter at the best of times. But no one told me the Viscontis are a pair of murdering, ruthless tyrants, famous all over Italy for their cruelty (hmmm, must have somehow slipped everyone's mind)!

Apparently, the first thing the vicious Viscontis did when they came to power was hold a hideous 40-day-long torture festival in which their enemies (i.e. anyone they didn't like) suffered eye-gougings, amputations and all sorts of other unspeakable horrors! I'll have to work out a way of being extra flattering to their stuck-up

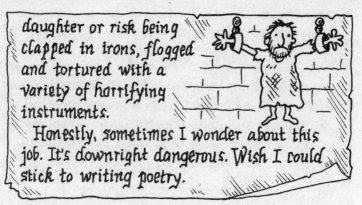

daughter or risk being clapped in irons, flogged and tortured with a variety of horrifying instruments.

Honestly, sometimes I wonder about this job. It's downright dangerous. Wish I could stick to writing poetry.

Geoffrey did get back from Lombardy in one piece. He was probably quite relieved that he spent most of his time in London. In 1374 he was given a job there as controller of taxes on the import and export of wool and leather. (Since wool was England's biggest export, this was a very important job.) With the job came some accommodation – Geoffrey lived above one of the city gates, Aldgate, and was allowed to stay there rent-free for life. As well as his salary from his tax job, he got some extra money from the King every year (as a sort of present, again for life), and he also received another gift for life from the King – a daily pitcher of wine. Since the pitcher held about 4.5 litres of wine, let's hope he didn't drink it all himself.

Geoffrey was now a wealthy man and he owned some very rare and expensive possessions…

...not diamonds, rubies, gold coins and that sort of thing, but books. Yes, books were so valuable in Geoffrey's time that they were chained to library shelves and only loaned out in return for a huge deposit. This was because there was no such thing as a printing press: every book had to be painstakingly handwritten. (Geoffrey's own poetry wasn't published in book form until after his death.) Geoffrey had 60 books of his own – the medieval equivalent of owning a Ferrari, except with extra points for being cultured.

As well as being rich, Geoffrey was well-connected: he was mates with John of Gaunt, Duke of Lancaster, who was the most powerful nobleman in the country, especially after Edward III became old and weak. It helped that Philippa, Geoffrey's wife, was lady-in-waiting to John's wife (the Queen, her previous employer, was dead by this time); and Philippa's sister, Katherine, was John's girlfriend and later his wife. (Nobody seemed bothered that he had a wife and a girlfriend at the same time.) Edward III died in 1377, and Richard II became King. Since Richard was only 11, someone was needed to rule in his place – and the obvious man for the job was John of Gaunt. So Geoffrey's pal was practically the King of England.

The tragic tale of Troilus and Cressida

By the 1380s, when Geoffrey was fortyish, he had a reputation as a poet: he would recite his poems himself, and they became a popular entertainment at the royal court. There's a famous picture of him reciting a poem to the King that looks a bit like this:

Geoffrey finished a long poem called *Troilus and Cressida* in 1383. Some people think it's his best one and it's been called 'the first novel in English', partly because the characters in the poem are complicated and believable, and develop over the course of the story (nothing written down had been like that before). The poem is set during the Trojan War and is a tragedy – a word Geoffrey used for the very first time in English. The tragic tale goes a bit like this:

THE CARTOON-STRIP TROILUS AND CRESSIDA

CRESSIDA IS A YOUNG TROJAN WOMAN ALONE IN TROY JUST BEFORE THE GREEKS DESTROY THE CITY. (HER FATHER HAS SWAPPED SIDES AND IS WITH THE GREEKS.)

SHE AND TROILUS, A TROJAN WARRIOR, FALL IN LOVE.

CRESSIDA IS TOLD SHE IS TO BE SENT TO HER FATHER IN THE GREEK CAMP IN EXCHANGE FOR THE RETURN OF SOME TROJAN PRISONERS.

TROILUS AND CRESSIDA PART, PROMISING TO BE FAITHFUL.

SNIFF   SNIFF

BUT WHEN CRESSIDA GETS TO THE GREEK CAMP, SHE STARTS A RELATIONSHIP WITH DIOMED, A GREEK WARRIOR!

TROILUS IS FURIOUS AND GOES ON A KILLING SPREE, UNTIL HE'S FINALLY KILLED HIMSELF.

More top jobs

As well as writing poems with unhappy plot lines, Geoffrey continued to work for King Richard II (although John of Gaunt still had the real power). He was made a Justice of the Peace in 1385, which meant he sat in judgment on minor crimes and did some of the work on more serious ones.

The following year Geoffrey decided that Aldgate was a bit too lively for him, so he moved to Greenwich – now it's part of London but in the Middle Ages it was outside the city in the Kent countryside. As well as being a JP, he was now made an MP – a Member of Parliament – for Kent.

In 1389 Richard II began to rule the country on his own (after all, he was 23 by this time). One of the first things he did was to appoint Geoffrey Clerk of the King's Works, which involved the administration of all the building works on Richard II's property. Being the King, Richard had quite a lot: a palace at Westminster, the Tower of London, a castle at Berkhamsted and no less than seven huge manor houses. So Geoffrey had a big job on his hands, with lots of responsibility...

The secret diary of Geoffrey Chaucer,
aged (roughly) 50½

Right, that's <u>it</u>. I can't take a <u>minute</u> more of this job. Everyone knows the Clerk of the King's Works carries lots of cash with him ... including every thief in England. I've just been robbed twice in the <u>same day!</u>

Maybe I'll give up work altogether and concentrate on my poems ... must say the latest one's coming along nicely. There are some great rude bits, if I say so myself.

Probably worn out by work and muggings, Geoffrey resigned from the job in 1391. He had other sources of income, including some that had been given to him for life by the King and John of Gaunt, so he could afford to.

The Canterbury Tales

The last poem that Geoffrey wrote is his most famous, although it was never finished. It's the first long poem in English that's about ordinary life. In case you don't fancy ploughing through about 18,000 lines of Middle English…

The cheat's guide to The Canterbury Tales

What's it about? In the General Prologue to the tales, we meet a group of people in a London inn who are about to set off on a religious pilgrimage to Canterbury (which was very much the done thing in the Middle Ages – religion was a big part of life). The group is made up of all sorts of different people – there's a knight, a housewife from Bath, a friar, a summoner (whose job was 'summoning' criminals to court), a monk, a parson, a physician, a cook and a miller, to name just a few (there are about 30). They decide that each of them will tell two tales as they ride on their journey to Canterbury, to help pass the time. The person who's judged to have told the best story will have his or her dinner paid for by the others when they get back.

Were they rather rude? The tales told by the pilgrims range from sad to funny to very rude indeed. Respectable people in the Middle Ages were allowed to be a lot more rude in public than people are today – laughing at dirty jokes was far more acceptable then. Here are one or two of the rude bits (for purely educational purposes, of course):

One of the funniest *and* rudest moments is when the summoner, who doesn't like the friar, gives his explanation of the special place in Hell reserved especially for friars – up the backside of the Devil himself!

In the Summoner's Tale, a nasty old friar who's trying to get his hands on an inheritance ends up with his hands on nothing but the dying man's loud and fulsome fart.

The Miller's Tale involves a young man kissing his beloved's bum in the dark, which she's stuck out of her bedroom window as a joke.

More than once Chaucer interrupts to 'apologize' for his characters' vulgar tales – he even says, 'I am a rude man'.

Was the poem popular? It's very unusual for manuscripts of poems to survive from Geoffrey's time, but more than 80 of *The Canterbury Tales* are

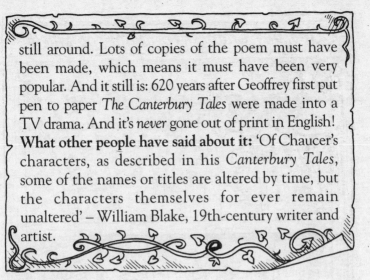

still around. Lots of copies of the poem must have been made, which means it must have been very popular. And it still is: 620 years after Geoffrey first put pen to paper *The Canterbury Tales* were made into a TV drama. And it's *never* gone out of print in English! **What other people have said about it:** 'Of Chaucer's characters, as described in his *Canterbury Tales*, some of the names or titles are altered by time, but the characters themselves for ever remain unaltered' – William Blake, 19th-century writer and artist.

The last verse

In 1398 Geoffrey left Greenwich and went back to live in London, in a house in the gardens of Westminster Abbey. The following year, King Richard II was forced to abdicate by the new king, Henry IV. Somehow, presumably using his tact and diplomacy, Geoffrey remained in favour with the new king just as he had been with the old: he still got his lifelong gifts of money and wine, plus some extra cash.

But Geoffrey wasn't to live at Westminster for very long. He died on 25 October 1400 – we don't know what of. At first he was buried in an ordinary grave, but 150 years later he was given the honour of a tombstone in Westminster Abbey. Usually you'd have to be a king or a queen to end up with a tomb there, but Geoffrey earned his place as a famous and well-loved writer. His tomb is in what's now known as Poets' Corner: Geoffrey Chaucer was the first of many horribly famous writers to be buried

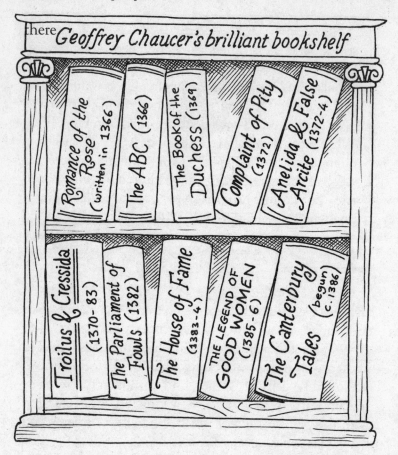

Geoffrey Chaucer's brilliant bookshelf

there

Romance of the Rose (written in 1366)

The ABC (1366)

The Book of the Duchess (1369)

Complaint of Pity (1372)

Anelida & False Arcite (1372-4)

Troilus & Cressida (1370-83)

The Parliament of Fowls (1382)

The House of Fame (1383-4)

THE LEGEND OF GOOD WOMEN (1385-6)

The Canterbury Tales (begun c.1386)

WILLIAM SHAKESPEARE AND HIS POPULAR PLAYS

William Shakespeare is the most famous writer of them all. For hundreds of years his plays have been performed all over the world in just about every language there is, on stage and film. Chances are you'll have heard of one or two of them:

MACBETH | KING LEAR | A MIDSUMMER NIGHT'S DREAM | HAMLET | OTHELLO

You might even have had to study them ... but don't let that put you off. William's plays were fantastically popular when he was alive and, the amazing thing is, they still are today. Of course, when William was born no one suspected for a minute that he'd be famous for ever...

Starting out in Stratford

William was born in 1564 on 23 April (at least, that's the most likely date) to John and Mary Shakespeare. He was the eldest of six children – four boys and two girls. John Shakespeare was a glove-maker, a respectable trade that meant the family was quite comfortable, but John was keen to do even better for himself and went on to become an important member of the town council ... before finding himself worse off than ever, as we'll see.

The family lived in Stratford-upon-Avon in Warwickshire, a small but busy town. Lots of people passed through Stratford in William's day, providing lots of passing trade for John Shakespeare's gloves. The town still has many of the buildings that William would have known when he was growing up, including the house where William was very likely born and which is now known as 'The Birthplace'.

WILL'S DAD

THE BIRTHPLACE

Creeping unwillingly to school

William was probably sent to 'petty school' at the age of five, where he was taught the alphabet and mastered the art of writing with a quill pen and ink – a lot trickier than writing with a biro. The sons of richer families would be sent to grammar school when they were about seven (nobody bothered about educating the daughters of any kind of family). We don't know for definite, but since John Shakespeare was doing very nicely for himself at the time, it's more than likely that William went to his local King Edward VI Grammar School.

Weekly King Edward VI School Timetable

	Early Morning		Late Morning		Afternoon
Monday	Grammar	B r e a k f a s t	Literature	L u n c h	Rhetoric *
Tuesday	Logic**		Divinity***		Latin
Wednesday	Latin		Ancient Greek		Music
Thursday	Geometry		History		Latin
Friday	Latin		Ancient Greek		Astronomy
Saturday	Arithmetic		Literature		Latin

* The art of persuasive speaking, Ancient Roman style.

** The art of reasoning, Ancient Roman style.

*** Religious Education, not Ancient Roman style (for obvious reasons).

Schools in Will's day clearly thought that Latin was a very good thing. It was still the language used in the Church, the law and medicine. The Ancient Romans were held in such high esteem that the school subjects were based on the Roman education system, and more or less all the literature learned at school was in Latin – by Roman poets, playwrights, historians and politicians. Some of the plays that William wrote later on took their plots and characters from Roman history or from Roman poets and playwrights.

The Shakespearean school day started early, at six or seven o'clock, and went on till five or six in the evening. You'll also have noticed that there was school on a Saturday as well as the weekdays. On Sundays there was no lounging about either – they were spent going to church and generally being holy. So there was hardly any time for fun. We don't know whether William was any good at his studies or whether he liked school. But he was almost certainly pretty worn out by it.

Boys usually stayed at school until about the age of 14, but it was probably a bit earlier than that for William, because John Shakespeare's circumstances took a turn for the worse in 1576. Although he'd been a council VIP in 1568–69, now John found himself in deep debt. If his dad had carried on doing well, Will might have gone on to university. As it was, he ended up working in the family business.

Will gets wed

In November 1582 William married Anne Hathaway, who was three months' pregnant with their first child. The unusual thing about Anne was that she was eight years older than Will – in those days 26 was an ancient age to be getting married.

Will and Anne's daughter, Susanna, was born in May 1583. She was followed two years later by twins Judith and Hamnet. The two girls lived long lives, married and had kids, but sadly Hamnet died when he was just 11.

We know that in 1585 William was welcoming his new son and daughter into the world, but then there's a bit of a blank until seven years later. All sorts of things have been suggested...

The truth is we just don't know. But the next time we do know what he was up to, he wasn't living in Stratford with Anne and the kids – he'd legged it to London.

The Tudor idea of fun

Theatre was an incredibly popular form of entertainment in William's day – it was the Tudor equivalent of the telly – so it's no wonder he was attracted to working in it. Will's first taste of theatre was probably watching Miracle Plays (with Christian subjects) when he was a child, and it's likely that he saw other sorts of plays performed by travelling theatre groups in Stratford, too. (We know John Shakespeare went to see the Queen's Men when they performed in Stratford, so maybe William, aged five, went too.) Since Will wanted to work in the theatre, there was really only one place for him to go...

The secret diary of
William Shakespeare,
aged (roughly) 23½

I've always luved plays - ever since I saw the Queen's Men (Qeen Lizzys own theeter groop!) when I was five. It's the only thing that reelly exites me. So I've dicided I HAVE to do sumthing about it. Im going to LONDON - where they have reel theeter

LONDON

buildings espeshly for putting on plays and nuthing else, the only ones in Englind! Londons THE place to be if you want to be a top riter or actor. Anne duznt seem so keen on the idear. But im sure she'll understand in the end – I've simply GOT to go!

We don't know exactly when Will went to London, of course, nor what his wife thought about it. But we do know he got there in the end, some time before 1592. Maybe Will joined one of the travelling groups of actors when he was in Stratford, or maybe he came to London and then joined a company of actors – once again, we don't really know.

Shakey spelling

By the way, if you're wondering whether William really was useless at spelling – yes, he was. He even spelled his own name lots of different ways. But then again everyone else was rubbish at spelling too, because there weren't any rules about it in those days, so it didn't really matter.

When he arrived in London, Will would have noticed that Tudor Londoners had other options for their spare time apart from going to see plays…

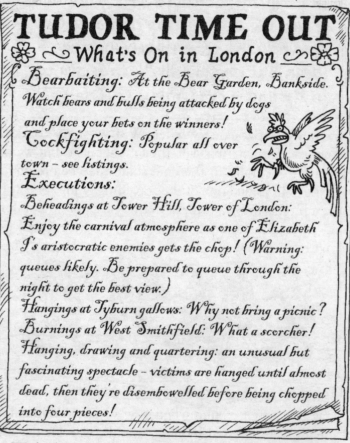

TUDOR TIME OUT
❀ What's On in London ❀

Bearbaiting: At the Bear Garden, Bankside. Watch bears and bulls being attacked by dogs and place your bets on the winners!

Cockfighting: Popular all over town – see listings.

Executions:

Beheadings at Tower Hill, Tower of London: Enjoy the carnival atmosphere as one of Elizabeth I's aristocratic enemies gets the chop! (Warning: queues likely. Be prepared to queue through the night to get the best view.)

Hangings at Tyburn gallows: Why not bring a picnic?

Burnings at West Smithfield: What a scorcher!

Hanging, drawing and quartering: an unusual but fascinating spectacle – victims are hanged until almost dead, then they're disembowelled before being chopped into four pieces!

With this sort of entertainment on offer, playwrights had their work cut out if they wanted to grab the attention of the average Tudor punter. Perhaps it's no wonder that one of William's first plays had an extremely gory story. In *Titus Andronicus*…

Tudor theatres

The very first building where plays were performed in London was the Red Lion Playhouse. In 1576 the first proper theatre was built in London's Shoreditch, called … The Theatre (how unimaginative is that?). Over the next 20 or so years several more were built, most of them on the south side of the River Thames at Bankside (handy for the Bear Garden – which itself became a theatre in 1614).

Theatres were doughnut-shaped, open to the sky in the middle, where the 'groundlings' stood to watch the play (not very comfy, but they only paid a penny to get in). A higher ticket price got you a seat in the gallery, and the real toffs could pay more and have a whole box to themselves. So it wasn't just one class of people who went along to the theatre – everyone went, they just had different seating arrangements. Modern theatre audiences are very quiet and well-behaved while a play is being performed, but in Will's day theatre-goers weren't like that at all: they would make lots of noise and heckle the

actors, and even throw rotten fruit and veg at them if they thought the play wasn't any good.

By 1592 William had a reputation as an actor and playwright in London. We know about that because another playwright at the time, Robert Greene, was jealous of William's success and wrote about him, describing him as an 'upstart crow'. Robert was particularly upset because he was posher and had a much better education than our Will, and was put out that someone who was lower down the social ladder should be more popular than him.

A theatrical theft

In 1598 Will's company of actors was finding it hard to pay the expensive ground rent on their theatre. The landlord who owned the land didn't own the building itself. So one snowy winter's night in 1598, Will and his mates took the whole theatre down, piece by piece, loaded it into boxes and took it to a spare bit of land in Southwark on the south bank of the Thames. Then they rebuilt the whole thing in just 28 days! They called it The Globe. Today, a modern reconstruction of The Globe on the South Bank stages William's plays as they would have been performed in his own time.

All of the roles in the plays were played by men and boys – no women allowed – so female roles were simply taken by boys wearing dresses. Some of the actors of Shakespeare's time became very famous: Richard Burbage was the most famous of Shakespeare's company. In a company like his, there'd be boy apprentices, hired men and 'sharers' – these were the actors (or playwrights in Will's case) who had shares in the business and stood to make some real money out of it.

Pesky Puritans, the plague and some sonnets

Desperately trying to spoil everybody's fun was a group of religious killjoys called the Puritans. They thought that plays distracted people from thinking holy thoughts and were therefore deeply sinful (actually, the Puritans thought most things were deeply sinful). When the plague made one of its periodic appearances, the Puritans saw it as evidence that people were being punished by God for doing deeply sinful things ... and watching plays came near the top of the list.

There were several Puritans on the council that ran London and so they banned all theatres within the city. But they only had power within the city walls, so theatre lovers got round the ban by simply building theatres outside the city walls, in places like Southwark and Shoreditch.

In 1593 there was a particularly nasty outbreak of plague. Theatres were closed down – even the ones outside the city walls – because people had cleverly started noticing that lots of bodies crowded together tended to make the disease spread faster, which was not a very good idea. The Puritans were also triumphantly saying that the plague was all the theatres' fault in the first place, of course.

By this time, William had written five or six plays but, with the ban on theatres, he was left twiddling his thumbs.

The secret diary of William
Shakespeare, aged 29½

It's SO BORING without the theeter.
Reminds me of beng back in
Stratford. A curse on the plaag (hope I
don't catch it – I've stuffed herbs in
me breeches so I'll probably be all
right). I've been spending (too much?)
time with some theetrical types.

WHEN are those comic actors going to velize that their own joaks just ARENT FUNNY??
 I was so boord the other day that I dashed off a long pome. It's called Venus and Adonis - about the goddess of love having the hots for a gorjous yung man. I think it's quit gude actualy. I cud do with some cash, so I'm sending it to Henry Rizzlie, the Earl of Southampton and an upperclass twit if ever there woz one. But he is loaded and I am hoping he will pay me for it.

William was right about Henry Wriothesley (pronounced *rizzly*, strangely enough) – he did pay him for *Venus and Adonis*. Will wrote another long poem for Wriothesley and loads of 14-line poems called sonnets – 154 of them to be exact. The sonnets are love poems, and they're where famous lines like…

Shall I compare thee to a summer's day?
Thou art more lovely and more temperate.

…come from.

By 1594 the plague was over – at least for the time being. William got together with some of his colleagues and formed a new acting group. All acting groups had to have the backing of a top toff otherwise they were classed as 'vagabonds' and could be punished. William's group was backed by the Lord Chamberlain and so they were called the Lord Chamberlain's Men. Will was to stay with them for 20 years, writing an average of two plays per year ... and becoming very rich in the process.

Will's popular plays

The Lord Chamberlain's Men's theatre, The Globe, became the most popular of its day. It's time to take a closer look at what made it such a hit...

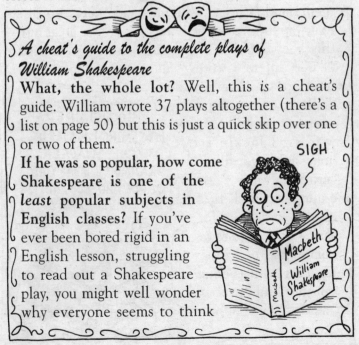

A cheat's guide to the complete plays of William Shakespeare

What, the whole lot? Well, this *is* a cheat's guide. William wrote 37 plays altogether (there's a list on page 50) but this is just a quick skip over one or two of them.

If he was so popular, how come Shakespeare is one of the *least* popular subjects in English classes? If you've ever been bored rigid in an English lesson, struggling to read out a Shakespeare play, you might well wonder why everyone seems to think

SIGH

Macbeth
William Shakespeare

he's so great. But the plays are written in the language of 400 years ago and were never designed to be read aloud in a classroom – or even read at all. They were meant to be acted on a stage. It's difficult not to get bogged down in the details of (to us) tricky language, so it's often a good idea to go and see the plays before you read them.

What's so great about them, then? William couldn't rely on complicated special effects or mood music to make his plays exciting and atmospheric, but he was so brilliant at using words that he didn't need them: he could (and still can) make audiences sad, happy, excited, terrified and generally spellbound. (Since William's audiences thought that watching someone hang or burn was great fun, this is even more of an achievement.) He used 18,000 different words – most writers only use a fraction of that number.

William even completely made up nearly 2,000 new words ('lacklustre', 'madcap', 'eyeball' and 'moonbeam', for example), and he's also responsible for some of the phrases we commonly use today (such as 'love is blind', 'in my mind's eye' and 'murder most foul').

BLOODSTAINED, BESMIRCH, MAJESTIC, OBSCENE, SWAGGER, TRANQUIL, IMPARTIAL, JADED, HOBNOB, HINT, LAUGHABLE, ZANY...

Will's Dictionary

Plus, the plays' themes are just as relevant to people now as they were to people in Tudor times. Here's a quick taste of the kind of things the plays were all about:

Romeo and Juliet: two young lovers whose families want to keep them apart – love, feuds, murder and suicide.

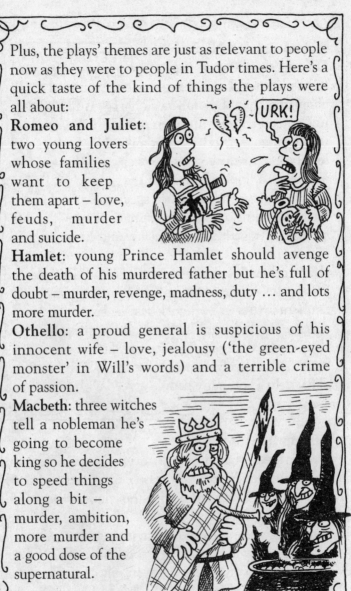

Hamlet: young Prince Hamlet should avenge the death of his murdered father but he's full of doubt – murder, revenge, madness, duty … and lots more murder.

Othello: a proud general is suspicious of his innocent wife – love, jealousy ('the green-eyed monster' in Will's words) and a terrible crime of passion.

Macbeth: three witches tell a nobleman he's going to become king so he decides to speed things along a bit – murder, ambition, more murder and a good dose of the supernatural.

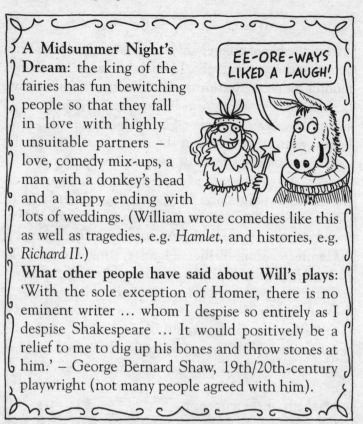

A Midsummer Night's Dream: the king of the fairies has fun bewitching people so that they fall in love with highly unsuitable partners – love, comedy mix-ups, a man with a donkey's head and a happy ending with lots of weddings. (William wrote comedies like this as well as tragedies, e.g. *Hamlet*, and histories, e.g. *Richard II*.)

What other people have said about Will's plays: 'With the sole exception of Homer, there is no eminent writer … whom I despise so entirely as I despise Shakespeare … It would positively be a relief to me to dig up his bones and throw stones at him.' – George Bernard Shaw, 19th/20th-century playwright (not many people agreed with him).

Queens and kings

Everyone loved the theatre … even Queen Elizabeth I herself. But Her Royal Maj wasn't expected to hoof it down to one of the theatres with the common herd – the actors came to her.

Queen Liz was quite fond of having people executed so it was important to be on her good side, whether you were a politician or a playwright. In July 1597 The Swan theatre staged a play called *The Isle of Dogs*. The play doesn't exist any more, but it must have been critical of the government or the royal court, because the government immediately closed it down, jailed all the actors and closed all the London theatres for several months for good measure. In fact, the play couldn't have been all that insulting or everyone involved in it would simply have been hanged or burned – perhaps with a little light torture thrown in. But the general message was: be careful what you write about the people in power.

Bearing this in mind, it was just a bit dangerous when the Lord Chamberlain's Men staged a performance of Will's *Richard II* a few years later. Queen Liz absolutely hated the play because it showed an English monarch being kicked off the throne. The Earl of Essex was planning a rebellion to get rid of Queen Liz and absolutely loved the play for exactly the same reason. He paid William and the rest of the company quite a bit of money to put on a performance of *Richard II* at The Globe the day before the planned rebellion, and got all his supporters to go along to it as a sort of pre-rebellion party. The Queen found Essex out and had him killed (of course). Henry Wriothesley, Will's patron, was also involved, but Liz took pity on him and simply had him thrown in the Tower of London for the rest of his life instead (which was good of her). The Lord Chamberlain's Men, including Will, were put on trial for their part in the proceedings. Thankfully, they got off. They must have been mightily relieved.

Queen Liz died just two years later, in 1603, and James I came to the throne. Luckily, it turned out that he liked plays. In fact, King James liked the theatre so much, and Will's plays in particular, that the Lord Chamberlain's Men now became the King's Men.

The secret diary of William Shakespeare, aged 39½

Now that King Jim's in charge Im difinitly NOT making the same mistaik twice (that terrible Richard II business nearly got us all killed!!). I know King Jim is a bit on the peculiar side and has a thing about wiches, wizzards and the soopernatural (bonkers if you ask me), and oviously hes Scottish. So to butter him up I've ritten a reely gude Scottish play all about witches and an ambishus nobleman cald Macbeth who murders the king (he gets his comeuppance in the end of course). And there's a speshul part for a good Scots noble called Banquo – who just happens to be King Jim's ancestor in reel life! I've kept it nice and short becos of the King's famus attenshun span (i.e. like a 2-year-old's). He's bownd to luve it!

James I did love *Macbeth*, and the King's Men were doing better than ever. They were even rich enough to buy the new Blackfriars Theatre, which meant they could stage plays indoors.

Will bows out

The fact that his plays were so popular made William a very wealthy man. By 1597 he was rich enough to buy a really flash house in Stratford-upon-Avon called New Place. You might have been wondering what had been going on with Will's wife and kids: we don't know how William divided his time, but one way or another he did stay in contact with Anne and the children, and after 1597 he stayed at New Place with the family when he wasn't in London. In about 1611 William made a break from London and the theatre and spent most of his time at New Place. Sadly you can't go and visit it today: in 1759 the house was bought and then demolished by the Reverend Francis Gastrell, who didn't like the theatre or people poking their noses into his back garden.

The last play Will wrote (apart from a couple that he co-wrote with another playwright) was *The Tempest*. William died on 23 April 1616, his 52nd birthday, and was buried at Holy Trinity church in Stratford. He'd had the foresight to write his own epitaph for his tombstone, which ends with the line 'curst be he that moves my bones' – and no one ever has dared to disturb the grave of the world's favourite writer.

QUITE RIGHT TOO!

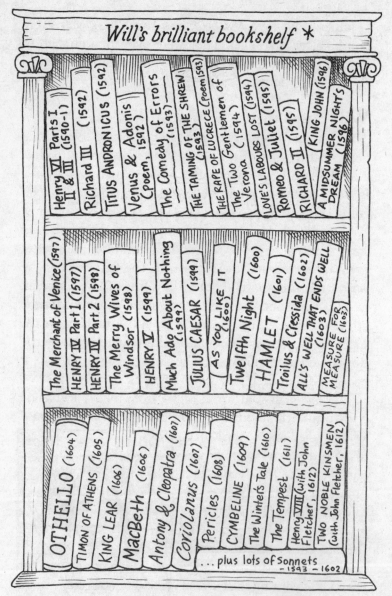

Will's brilliant bookshelf *

Henry VI Parts I II & III (1590-1)
Richard III (1592)
TITUS ANDRONICUS (1592)
Venus & Adonis (Poem, 1592)
The Comedy of Errors (1593)
THE TAMING OF THE SHREW (1593)
THE RAPE OF LUCRECE (Poem 1593)
The Two Gentlemen of Verona (1594)
LOVE'S LABOURS LOST (1594)
Romeo & Juliet (1595)
RICHARD II (1595)
KING JOHN (1596)
A MIDSUMMER NIGHT'S DREAM (1596)

The Merchant of Venice (1597)
HENRY IV Part 1 (1597)
HENRY IV Part 2 (1598)
The Merry Wives of Windsor (1598)
HENRY V (1599)
Much Ado About Nothing (1599)
JULIUS CAESAR (1599)
AS YOU LIKE IT (1600)
Twelfth Night (1600)
HAMLET (1601)
Troilus & Cressida (1602)
ALL'S WELL THAT ENDS WELL (1603)
MEASURE FOR MEASURE (1603)

OTHELLO (1604)
TIMON OF ATHENS (1605)
KING LEAR (1606)
MacBeth (1606)
Antony & Cleopatra (1607)
Coriolanus (1607)
Pericles (1608)
CYMBELINE (1609)
The Winter's Tale (1610)
The Tempest (1611)
Henry VIII (with John Fletcher, 1612)
TWO NOBLE KINSMEN (with John Fletcher, 1612)

...plus lots of sonnets
-1593 - 1602

* The first official collection of Will's plays was published in 1623.

JANE AUSTEN AND HER DASHING YOUNG MEN

Jane Austen's characters – headstrong young women, unbearable cads, interfering parents and, especially, dashing young men – are familiar to millions of modern readers and TV and film viewers. Two hundred years after she wrote about them, people still care about the marriage prospects of wealthy young people who only ever existed as figments of Jane's imagination…

LIZZIE BENNET FROM **PRIDE AND PREJUDICE!**

… AND MR DARCY!

SWOON

THE DASHING MR WILLOUGHBY FROM **SENSE AND SENSIBILITY!**

Jane Austen and her characters are famous now, but Jane's life wasn't full of drama and fame (although there were one or two dashing young men)…

Lots of Austens

Jane was born on 16 December 1775 in the village of Steventon, near Basingstoke in Hampshire. Her parents were George (a reverend) and Cassandra Austen, who both came from well-off families. George had been given a 'gentleman's education' (i.e. the best kind, ending up at Oxford University) and Cassandra was even more of a toff than her husband (one of her relatives was a duke). George was reverend of two parishes, which meant that the family had lots of money as well as a very nice rectory to live in.

Jane was the seventh of eight children:

JAMES (born 1765)

GEORGE (born 1766. Sadly, George had some kind of mental illness and was brought up away from home. He was hardly ever mentioned by the rest of the family.)

EDWARD (born 1767)

HENRY (born 1771)

CASSANDRA (born 1773)

FRANCIS (born 1774)

JANE (born 1775)

CHARLES (born 1779)

The Austens

Generally speaking, they all got on very well. But Jane's greatest friend was her only sister, Cassandra. They would remain the closest of chums all Jane's life.

School for girls

Boys were expected to do some kind of job when they grew up and so they were the ones who were given a 'proper' education. The Austen sons (except George) were all taught at home by Reverend Austen himself in butch, manly subjects such as Latin and Greek, until they were old enough to go either to university or into their chosen profession. But Jane and Cassandra were educated too: they were sent away to boarding school when they were aged seven and nine.

The girls were not very happy at the first school they were sent to, and became even less so when they contracted a horrible and dangerous illness – probably diphtheria (a contagious disease that starts out as a sore throat but can end up killing you). Luckily, they both recovered and were sent instead to the Abbey School in Reading, where they had a much better time.

Jane and Cassandra learned subjects including French, geography, music and drawing at the Abbey School, but none of it was taken particularly seriously – after all, they were only girls. The reason girls' education didn't matter so much was that they'd only be expected to do one thing when they grew up: get married and have children. (It's only rich girls we're talking about here: there was no school for poor girls *or* boys.)

How to get a good husband

Wanted: Posh Georgian Wife

Applications are invited from Young Ladies for the Post
of Respectable Wife and Mother.

Age: 21–29 (though 29's pushing it a bit to be honest).

Appearance: Handsomeness not essential but extremely
desirable (portrait appreciated).

Qualifications:

The applicant must come from a Respectable Family –
this is an essential Requirement.

Capital that will provide extra Income is desirable, but
other qualifications will be taken into account.

Knowledge of Cookery (though the servants will actually
be doing it, of course).

Basic ability to run a substantial Household, including
managing a team of Servants.

Proficiency in Needlework is essential, though plain work
will be carried out by servants.

Accomplishments such as Foreign Languages, Music and
Drawing are desirable but not essential.

Ladies of leisure

Once Jane had finished with her schooling, there was,
of course, no opportunity or expectation for her to earn a
living for herself (apart from by getting married, that is).
You might think this sounds wonderful … and in a way
you'd be right. Young women like Jane couldn't go off
travelling on their own or hanging around town with
their mates (neither of which would have been

respectable), but they could visit friends and relatives and go to dances (suitably accompanied), both of which Jane loved. There were plenty of other forms of entertainment, too:

- Playing cards, charades and other parlour games.
- Games of badminton.
- Walking and riding. (But definitely not hunting, shooting or anything *too* energetic.) Jane and Cassandra both loved walking.
- Music. Jane played the piano.
- Needlework. The Austen ladies did a lot of their own sewing and also made clothes for the poor. (There were rules about what kind of sewing you did when you received visitors – mending was considered common!)
- Writing letters. Jane especially enjoyed this. She'd often start a letter in the morning, and return to it throughout the day.
- Reading. The Austens owned a fair selection of books and the whole family read a lot. Jane enjoyed novels, poetry, Shakespeare's plays (which she saw performed sometimes, too), and also the popular Gothic horror stories and romances of the day, which were considered trashy and which Jane found very funny.

It might not sound a thrill-a-minute, but you have to admit that it could have been a *lot* worse: imagine the utter beastly ghastliness of having to work for a living, for example! Jane and Cassandra seem to have been very happy with their lives. And Jane had found another hobby: she started writing stories and plays as well as reading other people's.

Both Jane and Cassandra had a talent for humour and Jane's teenage writing was very funny. She wrote spoofs of popular romances, such as the tale of 'The Beautifull Cassandra', in which Cassandra shoplifts a hat and punches a cook. She even took on 'A History of England' but admits that it is 'by a partial, prejudiced and ignorant Historian' and it only contains one date.

By the time Jane was 21, she'd also written the first draft of a novel called *First Impressions*. Her father was terribly impressed and he wrote to a publishing company about it, but he didn't get a very encouraging reply…

The secret diary of Jane Austen, aged 21 ½

Father received a reply from the publishers today but when I asked to see it he made some excuse and would not show me. Later I sneaked a look and found out why. The so-called gentlemen at the publishing house had not even bothered to read my novel! They implied that they weren't interested because it was by a young

> woman and therefore bound
> to be literature of the lowest
> order! How frightfully rude.
> I have determined not to let it put me
> off. I am embarked upon my next
> novel. When I am a famous novelist I
> might write <u>them</u> an insulting letter!

By 1799 Jane had written two more manuscripts: *Susan* and *Elinor and Marianne*. To great excitement, in 1803 Jane sold *Susan* to a publisher for £10 – but disappointingly they never printed it. Much later Jane would revise and edit these early manuscripts and have them published as *Pride and Prejudice*, *Sense and Sensibility* and *Northanger Abbey* … but that wasn't for a while yet.

Dashing young men

As we've seen, the top priority for Georgian young ladies like Jane and Cassandra was to find a husband. Both of them were nice-looking and apparently attracted a number of dashing young men at the dances they went to. Based on the evidence of the letters she sent to friends and family that still exist, Jane seems to have been a bit of a flirt. But not all of her letters do exist: after Jane died, Cassandra went through them and carefully removed any references to anything that was private or that might have seemed inappropriate for a Georgian lady. Jane set tongues wagging with one gentleman, though: a young Irishman called Tom Lefroy seems to have had some kind of flirtation with Jane when she was about 20, but it couldn't have been very serious. There was another romance for Jane in 1798, with Reverend Samuel Blackall – but, whatever happened, they didn't end up getting married.

Cassandra got engaged to a clergyman called Thomas Fowle in 1795. He went to the West Indies as a regimental chaplain to earn some extra money before they married. Unfortunately, while he was there…

…he died of Yellow Fever. Cassandra never married.

There were, of course, other dashing young men in Jane's life: her brothers. They were doing much better at the business of getting wed: all of them married (except poor George who, sadly, we don't talk about). The eldest, James, married twice (his first wife died), and the most dashing, Henry, married his glamorous older cousin, Eliza, whose first husband got the chop in the French Revolution. Between them they produced various children, and Jane and Cassandra became very fond of their nieces and nephews.

All the brothers ended up respectable and quite rich, but Edward became the wealthiest of all. As a child he'd been sent to live with some relatives, the Knights, who had no children of their own. This sounds a bit odd to us today, but in those days it was quite common. The Knights were absolutely loaded and Edward stood to inherit huge amounts of money and property, including a whacking great mansion in Kent. He married an extremely posh woman.

Bath ... and some proposals

In 1800 the Reverend and Mrs Austen announced to Jane and Cassandra (the only two of their children still living with them) that they were to move to Bath. The rectory at Steventon would pass on to James because he was now a clergyman.

Jane was not pleased by the prospect of moving away from Steventon (there's a story that she fainted when her mother told her about it), but she determined to make the best of it. Bath was newly built when she went to live there and was very fashionable; but it didn't suit Jane, who preferred their old life in Hampshire.

In 1801 Mr and Mrs Austen, Jane and Cassandra went on holiday to Devon. While they were there, it seems that Jane fell in love. The details are very hazy because of Cassandra's letter-editing later on but apparently marriage was proposed. But then the man did something extremely inconsiderate, after which Jane couldn't possibly think of marrying him...

...he died.

Just over a year later, Jane received another proposal...

The secret diary of Jane Austen, aged 27½

I am about to do something I know I shan't regret, but that is one of the most difficult things I have ever done. Cassie and I have been staying with some dear friends at their house in Manydown. Last night — totally unexpectedly — their younger brother, Harris Bigg-Wither, announced his feelings for me and asked me to marry him! Then — also totally unexpectedly — I said yes! I can now see what a complete fool I've been. I have no real affection for Harris Bigg-Wither. It is flattering that he feels affection for me — he is a nice, wealthy young man, just 21, and I ... am not a young girl any more. I think for a moment my head was ruling my heart: I do not really want to be a spinster, but to marry without love would be wrong. It will be extremely

> embarrassing and hurtful but I shall have to tell Harris that I have changed my mind.
>
> It is wicked of me, but I must admit I have been thinking of the prospect of signing my name 'Mrs Harris Bigg-Wither'. That is another good reason to turn him down.

Even though she didn't love Mr Bigg-Wither and would have had to spend the rest of her life being called Mrs Bigg-Wither, marriage to Harris must have been quite a temptation for Jane who, at 27, was getting on a bit. There wasn't much in prospect for a single woman of Jane's class: all you could do was hope that one of your relatives was willing and wealthy enough to support you financially while you got on with your needlework. Not marrying and being an 'old maid' carried a stigma. In fact, the minute you married your status automatically increased. In Jane's novel *Pride and Prejudice*, the insufferably annoying Lydia Bennett, who has just got married, tells her older, unmarried sister at the dinner table:

> I take your place now, and you must go lower, because I am a married woman.

But despite this, Jane wasn't tempted enough and in fact she never married. In the same novel the heroine is told: 'Oh Lizzy! Do anything rather than marry without affection.' It's unlikely that Jane regretted her decision not to become Mrs Bigg-Wither.

A moving experience

In 1805 Jane's father died. Jane gave up on the writing she'd started the year before and wrote nothing at all for a few years after his death, which is perhaps a measure of how unhappy she was.

Mrs Austen and her two daughters were left with a reasonable income. They left Bath, which Jane was quite pleased about, and after a brief stay in Clifton they went to live in Southampton with their brother Francis and his new wife. Jane's good friend Martha Lloyd came to live with them, too. Francis was now a captain in the navy and his sisters were hugely proud of him. Mrs Austen, the two sisters, Francis and his wife and Martha all lived fairly happily together in Southampton for a couple of years.

In 1808 Edward Austen – the one with the mansion– had some sad news: his wife had died after giving birth to her 11th child. Cassandra immediately went to stay with Edward to help out while Jane looked after Edward's eldest two boys in Southampton. Edward was so grateful to his sisters that he gave them a rather large reward: one of his houses, in the Hampshire village of Chawton. The news that they were to leave an overcrowded house in Southampton, where they were getting under the feet of a young married couple, and move to a large cottage was very welcome indeed. The Austen ladies moved to Chawton in 1809.

Books by a lady

Mssrs Crosby, Publishers
Bath

Dear Sirs,
Might I remind you that six years ago you agreed to publish my novel, Susan? Would you mind jolly well getting on with it, please?
Yours sincerely,   Jane Austen

Miss Jane Austen
Chawton
Hampshire

Dear Miss Austen,
We purchased your 'novel' for £10. It is ours to do with as we please, and we are not disposed to publish it, causing possible damage to our reputation as fine and upstanding publishers of works of literary merit.
Pay us the £10 and you can have your work back. If you don't pay up and we find that it has been published by someone else, we'll have no hesitation in taking you to court.
So there.

     Mssrs Crosby

> *The secret diary of Jane Austen, aged 35½*
>
> *So, those pompous and insulting Messrs Crosby think they are going to receive ten pounds from me, do they, after accepting my manuscript for publication and then doing absolutely nothing whatsoever about it for six years? They will not receive one penny. I am revising the other manuscripts I wrote years ago – and they will be much better than Susan – and then they will be sorry! I shall be sending more than one publisher an insulting letter when my books are famous!*

Crosby

Jane did revise her earlier manuscripts and sent them off to another publisher for consideration. The first, *Sense and Sensibility* was published two years later. Jane didn't expect the book to do very well and had saved up some money to meet the expected loss, because she stood to lose money if the book sold badly. But in fact, Jane's writing career was off to a great start: the book was successful and she made a profit.

The story involves the marriage prospects of two young ladies...

THE CARTOON-STRIP
∽SENSE AND SENSIBILITY∾

UNMARRIED SISTERS, ELINOR AND MARIANNE, LIVE WITH THEIR MOTHER.

OUR BROTHER AND HIS SELFISH WIFE INHERITED ALL OUR FATHER'S WEALTH.

THEY LIVE IN OUR OLD HOME.

WE ARE FORCED TO LIVE IN REDUCED CIRCUMSTANCES!

ELINOR IS ATTRACTED TO HER BROTHER-IN-LAW, EDWARD FERRARS.

GOSH!

MARIANNE IS ATTRACTED TO THE DASHING MR WILLOUGHBY.

OOOH, WHAT A DISH!

BUT IT TURNS OUT THAT EDWARD IS SECRETLY ENGAGED TO SOMEONE ELSE!

ERM... YES. SORRY.

AND MR WILLOUGHBY TURNS OUT TO BE A BOUNDER AND A CAD!

WELL, IT'S TRUE I BEHAVED RATHER IMPROPERLY TOWARDS A YOUNG LADY. AND THEN I MARRIED PURELY FOR MONEY. BUT I REGRET IT! IT'S MARIANNE I LOVE!

TOUGH.

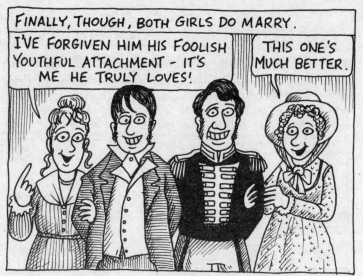

FINALLY, THOUGH, BOTH GIRLS DO MARRY.

I'VE FORGIVEN HIM HIS FOOLISH YOUTHFUL ATTACHMENT - IT'S ME HE TRULY LOVES!

THIS ONE'S MUCH BETTER.

Encouraged by the success of her first published novel, Jane spent most of her time at her writing desk in the front room of the cottage. But she kept her writing a secret. If anyone came to the house she would quickly hide what she was doing. The story goes that the living room where she wrote had a creaking door – she liked to keep it that way so that she'd have warning of anyone about to enter the room. Jane was secretive about her work because many people didn't think respectable ladies should go in for writing. There were all sorts of ways for a Georgian lady to be disapproved of, though this does seem one of the odder ones. If people had known about Jane's books she would probably have had to put up with all kinds of irritating nonsense so, perhaps wisely, she kept it to herself and a few friends and family. So *Sense and Sensibility* didn't have Jane's name on the front cover. In fact, it didn't mention her name anywhere at all, and neither did any of her other books – they all said they were 'by A Lady'.

Jane's next book was her revised version of the novel that had begun life as *First Impressions*. She sent it off to the publishers of *Sense and Sensibility*, who published it in 1813. The book had been given the new name of *Pride and Prejudice*, and became probably the best-loved of all Jane's novels.

A cheat's guide to Pride and Prejudice

What's it all about? In a word, marriage (which features heavily in all Jane's books). The novel's first line has become famous: 'It is a truth universally acknowledged, that a single man in possession of a good fortune, must be in want of a wife.' The Bennet family has five daughters, all of whom need to be married off (obviously). But the first impressions of the young women and the young men they meet are often proved to be wrong: in particular the spirited, unconventional Elizabeth Bennet's opinion of the dashing, rich Mr Darcy (who has been responsible for the most *phwoars* in the whole of English literature). By the end of the book a number of Bennet weddings have either already happened or are soon to take place ... but there are all sorts of complications along the way.

What other people have said about it: 'A very superior work. It depends not on any of the common

resources of novel writers, no drownings, no conflagrations, nor runaway horses … I really think it is the most probable book I have ever read.' – Annabella Milbanke (later Lady Byron), pointing out its difference from many of the improbably plotted novels of the time.

What Jane said about it:
Jane was delighted with *Pride and Prejudice* and called it 'my own darling child'.

Pride and Prejudice and *Sense and Sensibility* were both first written when Jane was much younger, but she also began completely new novels – *Mansfield Park*, *Emma* and *Persuasion* were all started and finished while she was living at Chawton. By 1815 she had four novels published, all of them doing well and making Jane a tidy profit. Jane finally decided that she would buy *Susan* back from the mean-spirited publisher, and it was published as *Northanger Abbey*. Sadly, she never saw it, nor *Persuasion*, in print.

A surprise ending

By the summer of 1815 Jane's health had begun to fail. The symptoms she suffered – tiredness, feeling sick, stomach upsets, weight loss and darkening of the skin – most likely point to Addison's disease. Today it can be treated, but in those days doctors didn't know what Jane's symptoms meant. Jane made light of her illness, perhaps because Mrs Austen was a terrible hypochondriac who moaned constantly about a long and varied list of minor ailments.

The illness didn't stop Jane from finishing *Persuasion* and preparing *Northanger Abbey* for publication. And in 1817 she was working on a new novel set in a seaside town called *Sanditon*. But she never finished it. She and Cassandra left the cottage at Chawton to stay in Winchester so that she could be near her doctor, but she died there on 18 July 1817, aged just 41. She was buried in Winchester Cathedral.

Persuasion and *Northanger Abbey* were both published after Jane died, adding to the brilliant bookshelf that finally made her famous.

CHARLES DICKENS
AND HIS ADORING FANS

Even if you've never read any of Charles Dickens's books, you've probably heard of some of them…

And you might also have heard things like…

70

Charles is still world-famous and he still has millions of admirers. But when he was alive he was practically worshipped by his adoring fans – just like some of today's A-list stars.

A star is born

Back in 1812, though, our Charles had only two adoring fans – his mum and dad (John and Elizabeth Dickens). He was born on 7 February in Portsea, just outside Portsmouth, where his father worked as a clerk in the Navy Pay Office. Charles John Huffam Dickens – to give our Charles his full and slightly strange name – was the second of six surviving children.

John and Elizabeth employed a young woman called Mary Weller to look after the little Dickenses. The bedtime tales Mary told the children weren't about Fluffy Bunny or Harry the Hedgehog; instead, they featured the aptly named Captain Murderer. Charles later wrote that Mary began her cosy story-times '... by clawing the air with both hands, and uttering a long low hollow groan.' The perfect babysitter, then. Mary's horribly scary tales of the man who made his wives into pies may have been the terrified Charles's first taste of the power of story-telling.

71

As he grew older he loved books – almost all of which he found a lot less frightening than Mary's stories.

The family moved around the south of England when Charles was very young, following John Dickens's different jobs for the Navy. In 1817, they settled for five years in Chatham, Kent, where John worked in the naval dockyard. Charles would look back on this period as the happiest part of his childhood. He was sent to school in Chatham in 1821, which he loved, but he didn't get to stay there long – when he was 11 the whole family moved again, this time to London.

Charles was not pleased to be taken away from Chatham But he was about to become a lot less pleased.

Debt and shoe polish
John Dickens didn't do badly out of his job with the Navy. But he must have had some rather expensive habits…

...sadly we don't know what they were, but we do know that John got into a serious amount of debt. As a way of finding some extra money for the family, his mum and dad sent poor Charles to work in a factory that made shoe polish (there was no law against child labour in those days).

The secret diary of Charles Dickens, aged 12

Only two years ago I was going to school in Chatham, playing with my brothers and sisters, reading books... I was happy. Now, I'm living in the most miserable city in the world, working in the most miserable, horrible, stinking factory in the world, doing the most miserable, filthy, noisy, smelly job in the world. My utterly vile employment is sealing up the jars of foul-smelling, revolting boot blacking and sticking on the labels. All this for six shillings a week!

Whenever I've thought about my future career, I never imagined this — I'm going to be a brilliant actor, not a factory worker! How I hate it here! Surely things can't get any worse?

Er – yes they could. Nowadays, when people get into too much debt they might get nasty letters from the bank. But in the 19th century, this is what happened…

John ended up in prison in Southwark, London, in 1824.

The secret diary of Charles Dickens, aged 12

11 days later.
Horror of horrors! Poor Dad and all that, but now that he's in the nick, how on earth am I EVER going to get out of this God-forsaken factory? The whole family has gone to live in the prison at Marshalsea - except me, of course, I'm staying at a flea-infested lodging house in Camden Town. I don't know which is worse. I have never been so miserable in my whole life.

A lucky escape

Charles's shoe-polish nightmare didn't last too much longer. John Dickens received an inheritance from his grandmother several months later.

HOORAY!

Incredibly, Elizabeth Dickens insisted that Charles should stay at the shoe-polish factory despite the change in family fortunes. (Charles never forgave her for this but he got a sort of revenge when he put her into one of his books as the silly, snobbish Mrs Nickleby.) However, John made sure his eldest son was soon out of work and back at school. Charles studied at Wellington House Academy for the next two years.

No doubt Charles realized that he'd had a lucky escape: he'd spent less than a year at the factory, but thousands of people worked in factories and lived in poverty their whole lives. Charles never forgot his grimy and unhappy time there, and the theme of Victorian society's injustices runs strongly through all his writing.

Back to work

Charles left school at 15 and started work as a clerk in a law firm. But he had always loved the theatre, and his real ambition was to be a comic actor. Never afraid of a bit of showing off, Charles would pay theatre managers to allow him to act on the stage in front of rowdy London audiences – a sort of Victorian form of work experience. Eventually he gave up on the idea of a career in acting, but he continued with amateur dramatics all his life.

Charles was always aware of the need to earn a decent amount of money – he wasn't about to end up in debtor's prison like his dad. He decided to learn shorthand and become a reporter in the law courts, since it paid better money than his job as a clerk, and Charles eventually became a parliamentary and newspaper reporter. But his true career hadn't yet begun.

Charles wrote short stories and essays in his spare time. When he was 21 his first story, 'A Dinner at Poplar Walk' was published in *Monthly Magazine*. Three years later, in 1836, his 'Sketches by Boz' were published. These 'sketches' were short stories about London lives, and became very popular. Newspapers started asking for more writing by 'Boz'.

Charles also wrote a comic novel called *The Pickwick Papers*, which was published as a book in 1836, the same year as 'Sketches by Boz'. A few months after he started *The Pickwick Papers*, Charles signed a contract with a publisher for his novel *Barnaby Rudge*. Although Charles continued to work as a newspaper reporter, his writing career was off to a flying start.

A romantic interlude

In 1835, Charles met Catherine Hogarth, the daughter of one of his newspaper colleagues, and the following year they were married. Catherine was pretty, quiet and gentle – just about the opposite of the outgoing, energetic, moody and ambitious Charles.

Charles and Catherine began their married life with a week's honeymoon in Kent. Then it was back home to a rented house in central London – quite a posh address, which Charles could afford because of the success of

The Pickwick Papers and 'Sketches by Boz'. The happy couple were to have TEN children together.

Charles and Catherine shared their home with Catherine's sister, Mary. Sadly, Mary died suddenly shortly after the Dickens's first child was born. Charles had been extremely fond of Mary, but his reaction to her death does seem a bit strange: he took a ring from her finger and wore it himself for the rest of his life; he kept Mary's clothing and would sometimes take it out to look at it; and he told everyone that he wanted to be buried in

Mary's grave (how would you have felt if you were Catherine?). In Charles's novels, the young, beautiful women who suffer tragic early deaths or other dreadful fates are probably an echo of Mary.

Lots and lots of books

Charles was full of confidence in his new writing career, and it wasn't long before his work became popular all over the world. In 1836 he gave up his job as a reporter and became editor of a monthly magazine called *Bentley's Miscellany*, which was full of short stories, serialized novels, poems and essays on all sorts of different subjects.

Of course, Charles continued to write his novels as well. All of them were published in serial form, in common with many other novels of the time, in magazines like the one he edited. In the days before Playstations, computers and the telly, people looked forward to the next instalment of a novel in the same way you might look forward to the next episode of your favourite soap. Instead of gathering round the telly, families would gather round while one person read aloud from the latest serial.

Charles's next novel, *Oliver Twist*, was serialized in *Bentley's Miscellany* beginning in 1837. Very briefly, the story goes a bit like this:

THE GANG'S STILL AFTER HIM...
BUT FINALLY THERE'S A HAPPY
ENDING: OLIVER FINDS OUT WHO
HIS PARENTS WERE, DISCOVERS HE
HAS AN INHERITANCE, AND LIVES
WITH MR BROWNLOW AND THE
MAYLIES HAPPILY EVER AFTER.

...AND FAGIN
GETS HIS
COMEUPPANCE
IN THE END TOO.

EEK!

Charles was becoming very famous indeed – and he was writing novels as if they were going out of fashion (which they most certainly weren't). Charles managed to churn out books at an incredible rate – sometimes he even had two of them on the go at once – and this was on top of other work like editing the magazine and writing essays. Added to that, Charles's books aren't exactly short: they're stonking great blockbusters.

CHARLES DICKENS

CHARLES DICKENS

Vicious Victorians

As we've seen, Charles had had a little taste of the viciousness of Victorian life, and it had made a big (and very unpleasant) impression. The Victorian poor had a pretty tough time of it, by anybody's standards. In those days, there was no help from the government for families who fell on hard times. Children were sent out to work (until 1842, children as young as seven worked down coal mines!) and had no right to education. People who had no means of earning money – who were sick, for example, and had no relatives to help them – would live in the most terrible poverty and could starve or die from the diseases that were rife in the slums. There were no doctors for those who couldn't afford to pay. The only 'help' available was the Workhouse, where the poorest of the poor were made to work hard in return for a meagre amount of food and shelter.

Armed with a keen sense of injustice, Charles would take long walks in London (he thought he should spend as much time walking as he did writing), and he was well known to lots of people, rich and poor, all over the capital. Charles wrote about his observations of London and other parts of the country in his journalism and in his novels. In 1838 he visited the famously horrible 'Yorkshire schools', where boys were neglected and beaten. Charles featured them in his novel *Nicholas*

Nickleby, in which pupils at Dotheboys Hall suffer at the hands of the abusive schoolmaster, Wackford Squeers. The hero of the novel, Nicholas Nickleby, has been employed as a teacher at the school and hates Squeers' brutality. As Squeers is about to beat another boy, Nicholas stands up to him:

> *Wretch, touch him at your peril! I will not stand by, and see it done. My blood is up, and I have the strength of ten such men as you. Look to yourself, for by Heaven I will not spare you, if you drive me on!*

The book led to the closure of several Yorkshire schools. In some ways Charles was a bit like the voice of the Victorians' conscience – and maybe that's another reason why he had so many fans.

Mr Popular

Charles wanted his work to appeal to as many people as possible, and he succeeded in becoming the most popular novelist of his age. Which is pretty impressive, you have to admit. Everyone seemed to love Charles Dickens, not only in Britain but all over the world. In 1842 Charles travelled to North America. If they'd had celebrity magazines in those days, Charles would definitely have been in them...

GOOD DAY! Magazine

Charles Dickens in Fashionable Boston

There's no doubt that Charles Dickens is just as popular on the other side of the pond as he is in Britain: the novelist, dressed in elegant English tweed, arrived in America for the first time this week and was beseiged by screaming Bostonian fans. The A-list penman beamed as his fans fell upon him. Some of them even snipped bits off his coat to take away as souvenirs! But the ever-popular novelist didn't seem to mind: he waved, smiled and signed autographs before being led away to his waiting carriage and plush hotel in Boston's fashionable centre.

Charles complained while he was in New York, 'If I turn into the street I am followed by a multitude.' But really he enjoyed being a celebrity. He gave readings from his work, but also took the opportunity to campaign for things like the abolition of slavery – which earned him some enemies, but plenty of friends, too. When he arrived home from America, English crowds cheered just as loudly to greet the returning hero.

Just as fan mail floods in for today's soap stars, Charles received cartloads of letters from his readers. While his novel *The Old Curiosity Shop* was being serialized, Charles got hundreds of letters about one favourite character in particular, a young girl who wasn't in the best of health…

The Charles Dickens Fan Club
Doughty Street, London.

Dear Sir,
I hope you will permit the impertinence of my humble missive. May I say what a great honour it is to personally address our country's most esteemed novelist.

To the matter at hand: my family and I have the immense pleasure of reading your splendid and affecting work, The Old Curiosity Shop, and await each episode with bated breath. I should like to express to you our deep affection for that beautiful and good child, your character Little Nell. But of late we fear for her. She is in poor health. You cannot imagine the sorrow & tears that accompany the contemplation of - alas! I can hardly bear to pen the words! - the death of Little Nell. (I have had to revive myself with smelling salts after writing the previous sentence.) Please, good sir, I implore you to spare her. I am not sure my dear wife could bear the grief.

I remain, Sir,
Your Most Humble Servant,

Harold B Sniveller Esq.

Charles showed no mercy, though, and ruthlessly killed off Little Nell. The instalment in which she bit the dust had the whole of Britain – and America – in floods of tears. Reading the passage on a train, the Irish politician Daniel O'Connell burst into tears and threw the magazine out of the window!

OH, POOR LITTLE NELL! I CAN'T BEAR IT! SOB!

Charles's books could make people laugh, too, and maybe it was this ability to mix comedy and tragedy, as well as unforgettable characters, that helped to make them so popular. One of his best-loved books uses some of the events in Charles's own life. Here's a slightly shortened version of it…

A cheat's guide to David Copperfield
Who's David Copperfield? The hero of the novel, a young child at the beginning, who's just a little bit similar to Charles Dickens himself.
What happens? As with all Charles's novels, quite a lot. Here are a few edited highlights:

• David Copperfield lives with his mum and horrible stepdad, Mr Murdstone. David's mum dies and Mr Murdstone takes David out of school and makes him go and work in a bottle factory (remind you of anyone?).

• David then lives with the down-at-heel Micawber family – David likes them but Mr Micawber is sent to debtor's prison (ring any bells?).

• David is adopted by his aunt, Betsey Trotwood. He finishes school and goes to work at a law firm (just like someone else we know).

• When the aunt faces financial ruin, David earns extra money by learning shorthand and becoming a newspaper reporter, and also writing stories for magazines (what a surprise).

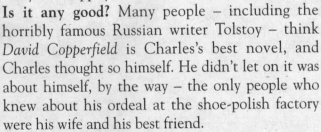

• Eventually, David becomes a famous writer (no, really?), travels abroad, and marries his childhood sweetheart. They live happily ever after.

Is it any good? Many people – including the horribly famous Russian writer Tolstoy – think *David Copperfield* is Charles's best novel, and Charles thought so himself. He didn't let on it was about himself, by the way – the only people who knew about his ordeal at the shoe-polish factory were his wife and his best friend.

What other people have said about it: 'There never were such people as the Micawbers, Peggotty and

Barkis, Traddles, Betsey Trotwood and Mr Dick, Uriah Heep and his mother. They are fantastic inventions of Dickens's exultant imagination ... you can never quite forget them.' – the English writer William Somerset Maugham.

What Charles said about it: 'Of all my books I like this the best.'

Travels and some sad events

Even though Charles was writing novels at a fantastic rate, wandering about the country documenting social ills, and editing a magazine, he still found time to travel abroad. In July 1843, the Dickens family (Charles, Catherine and four little Dickenses) set off for Genoa in Italy.

During this time Charles managed to knock out some Christmas stories, lots of journalism (especially travel writing), the whole of one whacking great novel (*Martin Chuzzlewit*) and the start of another (*Dombey and Son*). He certainly wasn't a slacker.

After the Dickenses had gone back to London to live, Charles started up a weekly magazine, called *Household Words*, in 1850. It was – surprise, surprise – hugely popular. As well as contributing to the magazine and editing it, Charles was also working on *David Copperfield*.

The secret diary of Charles Dickens, aged 38½

I've put Father into the novel I'm writing – he's Mr Micawber, who gets himself into debt and goes to jail. (You'd think by now I'd have forgotten that terrible time and the blacking factory – but I don't think I ever shall.) If I hadn't been able to pay off Father's debts over the years he would have ended

> *up in debtors' prison countless times!*
> *The old devil even borrowed money from*
> *my publishers, and I caught him selling*
> *my autograph and manuscripts*
> *to raise some cash! I wonder if*
> *he'll recognize himself in the*
> *book when it's published.*

Sadly, Charles never found out: his father died before he finished the novel.

Sadder still, Charles's baby daughter Dora had been very ill. Soon after John Dickens died, in April 1851, Dora died too. (Dora also features in *David Copperfield* – perhaps writing the book helped Charles in his grief for his father and daughter.) Devastated, the whole family moved to the Kent coast for a while. Charles decided that the house they rented in London was an unhappy place, and when they moved back to London it was to a different address.

By the 1850s, things weren't going so well between Charles and Catherine. They now had nine surviving children, but their marriage was coming to an end. Charles fell in love with a young actress called Ellen Ternan. Eventually, in 1858, he and Catherine separated and Charles moved permanently to Gad's Hill Place (a big country house in Chatham, Kent, that he'd bought a few years before). He and Ellen started a relationship but, this being Victorian England, it was kept very secret and no one knew at the time.

The last instalment

Charles began a series of readings of his work in 1858, which were instantly very popular (of course). The readings were a way of earning extra money (not that he needed it by this time), and allowed him to use his acting talents. Dickens gave more than 400 of these readings all over Britain, which often left him exhausted. He was now more famous and popular than ever.

Charles continued with his readings until 1869, when he reluctantly gave them up because of ill health. He began work on *The Mystery of Edwin Drood*. As he'd never written a mystery before, perhaps this would be a new direction for Charles's writing. Unfortunately, we'll never know: the book was never completed. Charles died suddenly at home on 9 June 1870, at the age of 58.

A special train brought Charles's body from Kent to London, and he was buried in Westminster Abbey. Thousands of fans came to say goodbye to Britain's best-loved writer.

Charles would probably have approved of the inscription on his tombstone in Poets' Corner:

'HE WAS A SYMPATHISER TO THE POOR, THE SUFFERING, AND THE OPPRESSED; AND BY HIS DEATH, ONE OF ENGLAND'S GREATEST WRITERS IS LOST TO THE WORLD.'

Charles Dickens's brilliant bookshelf

The Pickwick Papers (1836)

OLIVER TWIST (1837-8)

Nicholas Nickleby (1838-9)

THE OLD CURIOSITY SHOP (1840-1)

Barnaby Rudge (1841)

Martin Chuzzlewit (1843-4)

DOMBEY & SON (1846-8)

David Copperfield (1849-50)

BLEAK HOUSE (1852-3)

Hard Times (1854)

Little Dorrit (1856-7)

A TALE OF TWO CITIES (1859)

Great Expectations (1860-1)

Our Mutual Friend (1864-5)

The Mystery of EDWIN DROOD (UNFINISHED, 1870)

This bookshelf doesn't include any of Charles's short stories, plays, poems or journalism, and Charles also wrote five shorter length 'Christmas books' of which A Christmas Carol (1843) was the first and by far the most famous.

THE BRONTË SISTERS AND THEIR BOTHERSOME BROTHER

Sometimes, members of the same family all have the same talent – whether it's for tennis, trombone-playing or tiddlywinks. The most famous family of talented *writers* has to be the Brontës – Charlotte, Emily and Anne.

Oh, yes – and Branwell, the Brontë sisters' rather bothersome brother. Their story begins in the north of England...

Little Brontës

The Reverend Patrick Brontë was a parson, originally from County Down in Ireland, who began his career in various churches around West Yorkshire. He and his wife Maria had two daughters when they settled in the parish parsonage at Thornton, near Bradford, in 1815. By the time they left, five years later, their family had grown:

The Brontës were off to another Yorkshire town, Haworth. Today, the parsonage at Haworth is visited every year by more than 70,000 people, and is famous for being the place where the Brontë sisters grew up. It's a pretty place, set amongst the beautiful, rugged Yorkshire countryside. But in 1820, at the beginning of the

Industrial Revolution, Haworth was a mill town and life there could be grim: a dirty water supply and open sewers in the streets meant that the average life expectancy was only 25 years!

The Brontës weren't rich but they weren't poor either (they had a servant to look after them), which meant they were different from the other children nearby – too posh for the ordinary mill workers and not posh enough for the few rich families. So the Brontë children were isolated – there was no mixing with the lower orders in those days – and it was just as well there were six of them to keep one another company.

Some terrible news

Tragedy struck the family less than a year after their arrival in Haworth: Mrs Brontë became seriously ill. She suffered for seven months and died in September 1821– we don't know for sure what was wrong with her, but it was probably cancer. The eldest of the children was just seven years old.

With six unhappy children to look after, Patrick Brontë decided that desperate measures were necessary...

None of the women Patrick asked to marry him said yes. Instead, Elizabeth Branwell, Maria's sister, made the journey from her home in Cornwall to the Yorkshire moors, to look after her poor sister's family. She was known by the children as Aunt Branwell.

School ... and some more terrible news

For a few years Patrick educated his children himself. Even though most of them were mere girls and therefore not expected to know much, Patrick encouraged all the children to read novels, plays and poetry, and to find out about current events and politics. Patrick and the girls thought that Branwell was the genius of the family, though, and confidently expected him to go on to great things.

96

In 1824, the four eldest girls, Maria, Elizabeth, Charlotte and Emily, were sent to the Clergy Daughters' School at Cowan Bridge, a boarding school in Yorkshire. The teachers were harsh and strict, and the place was dreary and uncomfortable. The sisters hated it, but much worse was to come.

While they were at Cowan Bridge, Maria and Elizabeth both became ill. Maria returned home in February 1825; she died in May. Just a few weeks later, Elizabeth became ill and, tragically, she died too. The two girls had been killed by the disease tuberculosis (known in those days as consumption), which attacks the lungs. Nowadays it can be treated with drugs, but in the 1800s there was no cure.

It was only four years since Mrs Brontë had died. Now Charlotte, aged eight, was the eldest child.

Charlotte and Emily were sent home from the school and never returned, except in their imaginations. Much later, Charlotte used Cowan Bridge as a model for Lowood School in one of her novels, *Jane Eyre*. In the novel the disease typhus kills many of the pupils, including the heroine's dearly loved best friend…

> *When the typhus fever had fulfilled its mission of devastation at Lowood, it gradually disappeared... Inquiry was made into the origin of the scourge, and by degrees various facts came out which excited public indignation in a high degree. The unhealthy nature of the site; the quantity and quality of the children's food; the brackish, fetid water used in its preparation; the pupils' wretched clothing and accommodations – all these things were discovered.*

The land of fantasy

Patrick Brontë continued to educate the children himself. Most teachers at the time would have had strong views about suitable reading material for children, but Patrick let the little Brontës read more or less anything they liked: their Aunt Branwell's magazines, Shakespeare, the newspapers, fiction (including Jane Austen), and poetry. They also heard the most chilling of ghost stories, told by Tabby Ackroyd, a local woman who worked for the Brontës as a servant.

Maybe their wide reading habits and Tabby's spooky tales fired the children's imagination, because Charlotte, Emily, Anne and Branwell were soon making up their own stories. They told tales of adventure set in the children's own detailed and complicated imaginary world, which they called Angria. The children wrote several plays and lots of stories, making them into miniature books with tiny handwriting made to look like printed words. Since they had no other friends, the young Brontës' relationship with one another and the fantasy world they created together was very important. Because reality had so far proved cruel, perhaps the land of their imagination was a welcome escape.

In 1831, Charlotte was sent to a new school, Roe Head, which was 20 miles away and a lot posher than Cowan Bridge. She worked hard and did well at the school, and made some friends there. But she missed her brother and sisters and their imaginary land. When she returned to Haworth and the fantasy world (having learned all the school could teach her), it was to find a change in politics: Emily and Anne had split from Branwell and the kingdom of Angria; they now presided over the land of Gondal. Charlotte returned enthusiastically to Angria with her brother. She also had to teach her sisters what she'd learned at Roe Head school.

A grim life for governesses

In 1835, Charlotte was made an offer she couldn't refuse…

The secret diary of Charlotte Brontë, aged 19½

Roe Head has offered me a job. I've taken it.

I can't say I like teaching much but we can't all live on a parson's wages. <u>Someone's</u> got to do something and it looks as though it's got to be me. There's not much choice: it's either teaching or a low-class job like a maid's or a factory worker's, and of course I can't abide the thought of that. (Why are some professions, like the law or medicine, open only to men? It's not fair.) It also means that Emily and Anne can have free places to study here, so they'd better be grateful. (Why did I have to be the eldest?)

I'm going to keep thinking of other ways of earning money. There's some people born to be teachers - it's a pity I'm not one of them.

Silence!

In fact there was another option open to the sisters: marriage. But it wasn't one that they took; in fact Charlotte turned down two proposals of marriage, both in 1838. It looked as though the Brontë sisters were stuck with being governesses – either teaching the children of rich families and living in the same house, or working in schools. Unfortunately, all of them absolutely hated it.

Grim governesses			
Who	**Where**	**How long she lasted**	**Verdict**
Charlotte	Roe Head school	18 months 1831–32	Fairly ghastly, met some nice friends though
		20 months 1835–38	
	Sidgwick family	2 months 1839	Ghastly
	White family	10 months 1841	Ghastly
Emily	Miss Pratchett's school	about 6 months 1837	Ghastly
Anne	Ingram family	10 months 1839	Ghastly
	Robinson family	4 years 1841–45	Ghastly

There's a story that Emily's brief time at Miss Pratchett's school ended with her telling the children she liked the school dog much better than them! Anne had the most impressive stint, but that doesn't mean she was happy about it. Later on, her first novel was about a governess called Agnes Grey. Agnes's pupils consider her 'a hireling and a poor curate's daughter', and no one in the family she works for bothers to speak to her. She says:

> *It was disagreeable, too, to walk behind, and thus appear to acknowledge my own inferiority; for, in truth, I considered myself pretty nearly as good as the best of them, and wished them to know that I did so, and not to imagine that I looked upon myself as a mere domestic.*

Even though governesses were educated women, generally they were looked down on by their rich employers. That must have been hard to bear.

Bothersome Branwell

Being a bloke, Branwell had more of a choice of jobs. Unfortunately, he couldn't seem to find one that suited him. His real ambition was to be a writer, and he wrote to various publishers, poets and magazines throughout his life, without receiving any encouragement (usually not even a reply). He did manage to get some of his poems published in the local paper, but that was all.

Branwell first tried his hand at making a living from portrait painting in Bradford; he failed. Less romantically, he became a clerk for the new railways that were being built throughout the country; he was given the sack, suspected of nicking money. Then, while Anne was working for the Robinson family, Branwell joined her as a tutor, in 1843. He began a disastrous and scandalous relationship with Mrs Robinson, and as a result he was sacked in July 1845. Anne had left a month earlier, shocked by Branwell's behaviour.

After he'd been dismissed by the Robinsons, Branwell hit upon the idea of writing a novel. He called it *And the Weary Are at Rest*, and took its hero – Percy, Earl of Northangerland – from Branwell's childhood Angrian adventures. As well as writing the novel, Branwell also spent quite a lot of time drinking heavily and taking drugs. Maybe it was partly for that reason that his novel never found a publisher.

Branwell was always getting into drunken scrapes, some of them very dangerous indeed. Once he set fire to his bedclothes while in a drunken stupor and Emily saved him by putting out the flames with her bare hands.

The Brontë sisters' school scheme

Since they were less than happy about being governesses at schools or for wealthy families, the Brontë sisters came up with another idea…

The secret diary of Charlotte Brontë
aged 25

Right. We've all done stints as governesses and teachers - months of it - and we've mostly hated it. Try as I might I can't think of another way of earning money. So I've decided: why work for someone else? We're setting up our own school.

We need to learn languages if we're to do that, and I've decided we have to go and study French and German in Brussels. I found out Aunt Branwell has enough money to send two of us and I've convinced her to come up with the cash for me and Emily. (How would anything get done around here if it weren't for me?) I've told her it'll be worth it in the end and I'm going to work as hard as I can. Emily will do the same, if she knows what's good for her.

Charlotte and Emily travelled to Brussels in February 1842 to study French and German in a language school called the Pensionnat Heger.

Elizabeth Branwell died in November 1842, so the sisters returned home for their aunt's funeral. Charlotte went back to Brusssels in January 1843, but Emily decided to stay at home. Charlotte was given a job teaching English at the Pensionnat Heger and she paid for German lessons out of her salary. But there was another reason Charlotte wanted to go back to the school in Brussels: she had fallen in love with Monsieur Heger, who ran the school.

Unfortunately, there was something standing in the way of Charlotte's grand passion:

OUI! C'EST MOI – MADAME HEGER!!!

Rather unwisely, Charlotte had sent Monsieur Heger some love letters while she'd been in England. Monsieur Heger had torn the letters up and thrown them in the bin. But his wife had fished them out and stitched them back together with thread! The general tone of the letters was a little bit like this:

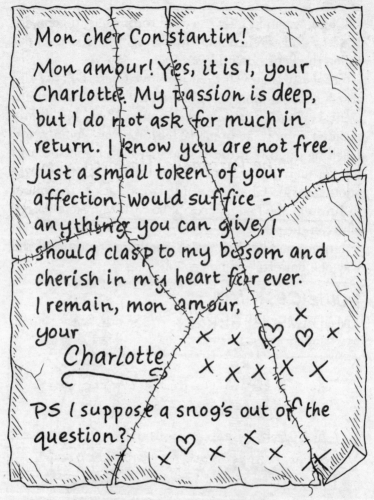

Mon cher Constantin!

Mon amour! Yes, it is I, your Charlotte. My passion is deep, but I do not ask for much in return. I know you are not free. Just a small token of your affection would suffice - anything you can give, I should clasp to my bosom and cherish in my heart for ever. I remain, mon amour, your

Charlotte

PS I suppose a snog's out of the question?

So Charlotte's reception in Brussels was frosty, to say the least. It seems incredible but, despite this, she stayed there a whole year before returning to Haworth … and the prospect of life without Monsieur Heger.

In 1844, with Charlotte back from Brussels, the girls set about producing leaflets for their new school:

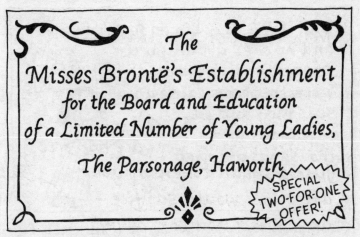

They received not one reply. The idea of the school had to be given up.

Published poets

The Brontë sisters had to think of another way to help the family fortunes…

The secret diary of Charlotte Brontë, aged 28

Last week I found some of Emily's poetry. It's not bad. In fact, it's good. I've written some poems too, and so has Anne - the solution to our money trouble is obvious! We must collect the best ones altogether and get them published. Emily caused a fuss but I told her to stop mithering and get on

with it. We've got to do <u>something</u> — and no one's got any better suggestions. Anyway, when the poems cause a sensation and sell thousands and thousands of copies, we'll be rich!

In May 1846, *Poems* by Currer (Charlotte), Ellis (Emily) and Acton (Anne) Bell was published at the authors' expense (the money came from Aunt Branwell's legacy). The sisters had decided to use the pen names instead of their real ones so that they wouldn't be identified as women. There was still a certain amount of prejudice about women authors: ten years earlier, on her Christmas holiday from Roe Head, Charlotte had written to the Poet Laureate, Robert Southey, enclosing some of her poems. She received a reply in which he said:

Literature cannot be the business of a woman's life, and ought not to be.

Robert Southey's views were a bit old-fashioned even for the 1830s, but the sisters didn't want people's ideas about women to influence their judgement of the poems. However, they needn't have worried: *Poems* sold, in total, a measly *two* copies.

A novel scheme

Undaunted by the less than blistering success of *Poems*,
Charlotte came up with a new scheme…

The secret diary of Charlotte Brontë,
aged 29 ½

Right. So the school was a failure and so
were the poems, I'll admit that. But I've
come up with another idea: Branwell's
writing some kind of
novel and if he can
do it so can we: me,
Emily and Anne
are going to write a
novel each and this
time we <u>shall</u> make our
fortune. We've always written stories,
ever since we were children, so it
shouldn't be too difficult. Emily and
Anne looked a bit unsure at first but I
gave them one of my hard
stares and handed out the
pens. I've given us a
deadline of ten weeks -
that should be more than
enough to bash out a quick bestseller.
This time next year we'll be rich!

my
book
by
me

Within just two months, by the summer of 1846, Emily's *Wuthering Heights*, Anne's *Agnes Grey* and Charlotte's *The Professor* were all complete. The three manuscripts were sent off and, after a few rejections, a London publisher accepted *Wuthering Heights* and *Agnes Grey*. Charlotte's *The Professor* continued on its lonely way around other publishing houses. Finally, she sent off a new novel, *Jane Eyre*, that *was* accepted by a publisher – it was published in October 1847 and *Wuthering Heights* and *Agnes Grey* came out in December the same year. Roughly 18 months after they'd come up with the idea, the three sisters were published authors.

A cheat's guide to the Brontës' books

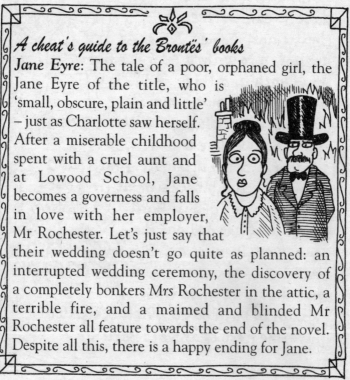

Jane Eyre: The tale of a poor, orphaned girl, the Jane Eyre of the title, who is 'small, obscure, plain and little' – just as Charlotte saw herself. After a miserable childhood spent with a cruel aunt and at Lowood School, Jane becomes a governess and falls in love with her employer, Mr Rochester. Let's just say that their wedding doesn't go quite as planned: an interrupted wedding ceremony, the discovery of a completely bonkers Mrs Rochester in the attic, a terrible fire, and a maimed and blinded Mr Rochester all feature towards the end of the novel. Despite all this, there is a happy ending for Jane.

Charlotte went on to write two more novels, *Shirley* and *Villette*, but *Jane Eyre* remains the most popular.

Wuthering Heights: 'Wuthering Heights' is the name of the house where Catherine Earnshaw, her brother Hindley, and their mysterious step-brother, Heathcliff, live. Hindley and Heathcliff hate each other but Heathcliff and Cathy are inseparable as children and share a passionate love: Cathy says, 'He's more myself than I am. Whatever our souls are made of, his and mine are the same' … but all the same she marries a rich neighbour, Edgar Linton, and Heathcliff disappears. When he returns three years later, now a wealthy man, he gradually takes control of both Wuthering Heights and Edgar Linton's house, destroying the lives of just about everybody else in the process, with his love for Cathy at the centre of it all.

The novel is a complicated, powerful mixture of passionate lurve, jealousy, revenge, violence, death and a particularly scary ghost … with maybe a glimmer of hope for the future.

It's Emily's only novel (for reasons which will become clear on page 114), but it has continued to enthral readers for more than 150 years.

Agnes Grey: We met Agnes on page 102, a governess who's the daughter of a clergyman – er, a bit like the book's author. She is badly treated and humiliated by her employers, but ends up happy and married to a decent man – unlike Agnes's wealthy but unpleasant pupil, Rosalie, who ends up very unhappy and married to a horrible man. And serve her right.

Anne went on to write *The Tenant of Wildfell Hall*, in which the drunken, violent Arthur Huntingdon is based on bothersome Branwell.

All three books by the Bell 'brothers' got noticed, but it was *Jane Eyre* that became a bestseller.

There was a lot of speculation about the Bells. Who were they? Were the books, in fact, the work of just one author using three different names? For the time being, Charlotte, Emily and Anne kept quiet.

Probably because of *Jane Eyre*'s success, the publisher of Emily's and Anne's novels tried to suggest that the new book by Anne, *The Tenant of Wildfell Hall*, was the work of the most successful 'brother', Currer Bell. Deciding that 'Acton Bell's publisher is a shuffling scamp', Charlotte and Anne set off for London to set the record straight and arrived at Charlotte's publishers, Elder & Co. Their secret was out.

Lots of really terrible news

Meanwhile, Branwell had received some news – Mr Robinson (his old employer and husband of the woman he loved) was dead.

Sadly, that's not how things turned out. Maybe Lydia made up the story, but she told Branwell that her husband's will specified that if she saw Branwell (let alone married him) she would inherit nothing, and she promptly married someone else. Branwell sank even further into depression. Lydia sent him money – maybe out of guilt – which he spent on drink and drugs.

Keeping himself healthy wasn't a top priority, and Branwell contracted tuberculosis and died in September 1848, at the age of 30.

Branwell's funeral was the last time Emily left the house. She got tuberculosis too, and died three months later.

Just a few weeks later, Anne began showing the all-too-familiar tuberculosis symptoms:

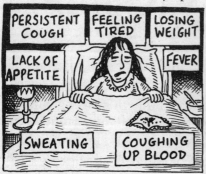

Anne wanted to go to her favourite seaside place, Scarborough, before she died. She got her wish, and died at Scarborough in May 1849. Like Emily, she was dead before her 30th birthday.

Fame and proposals

Charlotte finished her new novel, *Shirley*, after Anne's death. When it was published late in 1849, Charlotte made the journey to London to her publishers. Finally, Charlotte (rather than Currer Bell) was a famous writer – and she was introduced to other famous writers, such as William Thackeray (whom she described as 'very ugly indeed') and Elizabeth Gaskell (who later wrote a biography of Charlotte). In 1850, Charlotte also completed the 'painful and depressing' task of editing her sisters' work and writing biographical notes for their books.

Later the same year James Taylor, who worked for her publisher, asked Charlotte to marry him. She was not keen, however (this makes three marriage proposals she's refused, if you're counting), and the disappointed Mr Taylor went off to work in India.

In 1852, the curate at the Haworth parsonage, the Reverend Arthur Bell Nicholls, proposed marriage to Charlotte. Patrick Brontë was very much against the idea, and Charlotte refused, partly because of her dad's views on the subject. The Reverends Nicholls and Brontë were now furious with each other. Arthur left Haworth in May 1853, but he and Charlotte kept in touch. Charlotte's dad gradually became less grumpy about Arthur and the idea of a wedding. Finally, in April 1854 Arthur Nicholls returned to Haworth. On 29 June 1854…

Charlotte had finally said yes.

Yet more terrible news

It seems that Charlotte was happy with the Reverend Nicholls, but the Brontës had had a few years without any terrible news, so something appalling was almost bound to happen. And it did. Less than a year later, Charlotte died. No one is sure exactly what she died of, but she was expecting a baby and it was probably some kind of complication with the pregnancy.

Poor Patrick had buried all six of his children. He survived until 1861, reaching the grand age of 84. Arthur didn't marry again. He died in 1906, having seen his wife's and her sisters' books enjoyed by generations of readers.

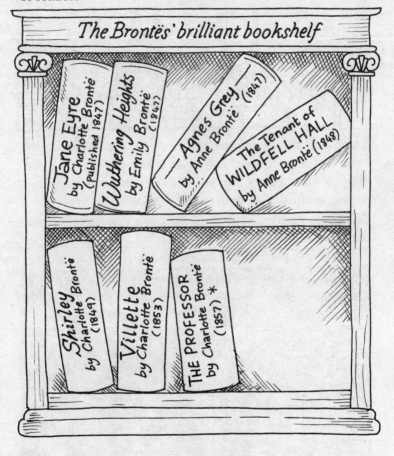

The Brontës' brilliant bookshelf

Jane Eyre by Charlotte Brontë (published 1847)

Wuthering Heights by Emily Brontë (1847)

Agnes Grey by Anne Brontë (1847)

The Tenant of WILDFELL HALL by Anne Brontë (1848)

Shirley by Charlotte Brontë (1849)

Villette by Charlotte Brontë (1853)

THE PROFESSOR by Charlotte Brontë (1857) *

* The very first novel Charlotte wrote was published two years after she died.

THOMAS HARDY AND HIS WESSEX

Thomas Hardy is famous for novels that are all set in the beautiful area of southern England where he was born. (If you go there today you can't turn round without seeing some sort of reference to Thomas or his books.) So it's probably just as well he wasn't born in a semi-detached house in Milton Keynes.

Some of Thomas's books are also famously tragic…

We'll find out about them later on. First, let's turn to the beginning of Thomas's own story.

A bad beginning

Thomas was born on 2 June 1840 in the hamlet of Higher Bockhampton in the Dorset countryside. But young Thomas didn't get off to a very good start:

As he grew older, Thomas was a bit of a weakling physically, but at least no one mistook him for being dead.

Thomas's dad (another Thomas) was a stonemason and master builder. Building had been the family trade for years, and in fact our Thomas's grandfather had built the cottage where they lived. His mum, Jemima, had been a servant in a rich household before she got married, and was now concentrating on having children – the couple had three more after Thomas. Although they weren't rich, the Hardys were fairly well off and could afford to send their children to school. It must have been a bit irritating for young Thomas to be kept at home because of his health while some of his younger siblings went to school. But this didn't stop him from learning to read earlier than most kids and taking up the violin.

School at last

When he was eight Thomas was fit enough to be sent to the village school, where he stayed for a year before being sent to a new school, a five-kilometre walk away in the town of Dorchester.

Thomas liked the school and did well there straight away – so much so that he was awarded a special treat:

After a couple of years, the schoolmaster opened the more advanced 'Academy', where the rest of Thomas's school life was spent. The subjects he was taught there sound just a bit on the dull side – Latin, maths, elementary drawing and nothing else – but somehow Thomas managed to enjoy them. He made up for the lack of variety by learning French and German and reading Shakespeare (among other writers) outside school.

You couldn't accuse Thomas Hardy of being a sulky, badly behaved teenager. When he wasn't at school or reading he was involved in the family passion for music. Thomas and his father would play the fiddle at weddings and other events. They played for free as a favour to their neighbours, and had such a good reputation that they were very much in demand. It wasn't a case of just banging out a song or two – at times, father and son (and sometimes other relatives too) would play for six or seven hours and then have to trudge miles home in the early morning.

Architecture and ancient Greek

The secret diary of Thomas Hardy, aged 16 ¼

It's time to say goodbye to the Academy. I'm going to miss my friends. And Latin. And I'm giving up the French lessons I've been having outside school. Still, I always knew it couldn't go on for ever and I'm sure I can find the time to carry on with some Latin, just for fun. In a few days I'm going to work for an architect called John Hicks, someone my dad knows in Dorchester. I'll be an apprentice for three years, then I'll be a qualified architect!

Two months later
A lot of the firm's work is restoring beautiful old churches, which I'm enjoying.

> And I've become friends with one of the other apprentices, Bastow - we're having a great time together: he's a big fan of Latin and Greek, so we're reading some Latin classics, and I've started learning ancient Greek. What fun! I'm looking forward to reading Greek drama in its original language - the tragedies are my favourites.
>
> It's hard to find time for it all but I can just about fit it all in if I get up at six o'clock and, if Dad and me are playing at a wedding party, go to bed at two.

Thomas lost his wild companion when Bastow emigrated to Tasmania in 1860, but he kept up with his studies for quite a while. Eventually, though, he realized that he couldn't carry on learning to be an architect as well as studying ancient languages. Even his mate Horace Moule (who was an enthusiastic student of Latin and Greek) advised him to concentrate on his career.

While he was working for John Hicks, some of Thomas's writing was published for the first time, in a local newspaper. The first publication was a funny article about a Dorchester clock, written in the form of a letter from the ghost of the clock (well, we've all got to start somewhere). Then his poem 'Domicilium' was published (about the cottage where he was born), as well as several articles about church restorations by his firm of architects.

Pongs and poetry

Eventually, Thomas's apprenticeship was over. It was time to find a job as a qualified architect, and Thomas landed a very good one, working for Arthur Blomfield, a well-respected London architect. Part of Thomas's work was supervising the digging up of bodies from London churchyards to make way for the new railways. You can see one of the old graveyards he worked on at St Pancras Old Church – Thomas arranged the old gravestones in a rather fetching circular pattern and planted a tree in the middle, which is now known as Hardy's tree. But as well as the artistic arrangement of gravestones, Thomas had another passion...

The secret diary of Thomas Hardy, aged 23½

'I've been writing poetry and sending it off to magazines and journals for years now. No one wants to publish it. The only thing I did get published was that stupid article called 'How I Built Myself a House' in Chambers Journal (and those articles and the poem when

I was much younger). I'm never going to see my poems in print at this rate.

London stinks. Quite literally. Not that long ago (1858) they had a summer everyone called The Great Stink - the House of Commons at Westminster had to hang sacking soaked in chemicals out of the windows so that the foul pong didn't overcome the MPs! It's that disgusting, sewage-filled River Thames. What with that and the smogs, I'm feeling ill all the time.

What am I doing in this horrible, unhealthy place? And am I <u>ever</u> going to be a published writer?

Back to Dorset

Thomas decided to leave London and go back to the Dorset countryside in 1867. After a few weeks' staying at his parents' house and working for John Hicks again, his health was much better.

Thomas was a practical sort of bloke, and instead of brooding for too long, he accepted that he'd never be able to make a living from writing poetry (what with the fact that not one of his poems had been published). So, instead, he began to try a different kind of writing: he started on a novel called *The Poor Man and the Lady*. By June 1868 he had finished it and sent it off to a publisher.

Very quickly, Thomas did much better than he had in the years he'd been sending out his poetry. He had an encouraging letter from one publisher, Alexander Macmillan, who eventually decided *The Poor Man and the Lady* wasn't quite good enough, but put Thomas in touch with another publisher, Frederick Chapman, because he thought he might be the best person to help Thomas with his writing.

> **The secret diary of Thomas Hardy, aged 28 ¾**
>
> Just had a meeting with none other than George Meredith - the famous novelist! - who's been working for Frederick Chapman reading his manuscripts. Although they were going to publish, Meredith has suggested to me that I am capable of a lot better and thinks I shouldn't publish but start on something else instead. It's disappointing, but not nearly so

> disappointing as all those years
> sending off my poetry with hardly any
> response! And I think Meredith is right:
> I <u>can</u> do better. I'm starting on a new
> novel right now. I've decided it's going
> to be a tragedy - after all, that's what
> human life is all about. Hurray!

Thomas's new novel was called *Desperate Remedies*, and in March 1870 Thomas sent the manuscript off to Alexander Macmillan.

Meanwhile, Thomas continued to work as an architect in Dorset. John Hicks had died, and Thomas was now living and working for a different architect in Weymouth.

Tom's totty

Just after he'd sent off his new novel, Thomas agreed to do some church restoration work in Cornwall for the Weymouth architect, and set off for St Juliot, near Boscastle.

> **The secret diary of Thomas Hardy,**
> **aged 29¾**
>
> I've just got back from the Rectory at
> St Juliot's. Terribly interesting Norman
> arches. But even more interesting was
> Emma Gifford, the Rector's sister-in-
> law. We went for several long walks

and horse rides and I must admit I was wishing like mad that her sister wasn't there. I've even written a poem about meeting her. Golly.

I think I should return to St Juliot's as soon as possible - to carry on with the restoration work, obviously.

We don't know the details of Thomas's love life, but he does seem to have been a bit of a one for the ladies. By this point in his life, Thomas had already been in love with or had relationships with at least the following list of lovelies:

• Lizbie Browne (one of Thomas's first loves, who scorned him)
• Someone called Louisa (it seems that Thomas carried on seeing her for a few years)
• Cassie Pole
• Eliza Nichols
• Tryphena Sparks

All of them were Dorset girls – maybe we just don't know about the London branch of Tom's love life. But perhaps the most serious love interest of all was the delightfully named Tryphena Sparks, who was Thomas's cousin. He had started seeing her in 1867, and he might even have been engaged to her. Rather naughtily, he was probably still seeing Tryphena even after he'd started seeing Emma down in Cornwall.

Perhaps for that reason, Thomas's relationship with Emma wasn't exactly a whirlwind romance – he would go down to Cornwall to see her two or three times a year. But eventually, on 17 September 1874…

St Peter's Church Paddington

Four and a half years after they'd met, Thomas and Emma were married in London (where they then lived for a while) in a very quiet ceremony. This was partly because their two families didn't get on at all well – especially Emma's and Thomas's mothers.

Success at last

Meanwhile, Thomas was busy working as an architect and writing. Macmillan had decided not to publish *Desperate Remedies* because it was 'sensational' (in it an unmarried woman has a child – they were easily shocked in those days). But a different publisher did agree to publish it. Thomas took a bit of a risk because the publishers demanded that he should invest £75 of his own money, which he stood to lose if the book didn't sell very well – at the time this was a *lot* of money. Thomas only had about £120 in the world.

Desperate Remedies was published, anonymously, in 1871 ... and it didn't sell very well. To add insult to injury, there was a terrible review in the *Spectator* that sounded a bit like this:

Good heavens! I'm so appalled by this novel that I can't quite bring myself to say why! The writer and publisher should be utterly ashamed

Luckily, Thomas wasn't too discouraged and decided to continue with his writing.

Reviews of *Desperate Remedies* were generally pretty bad, but some of them had praised the descriptions of the countryside and country life. This prompted Thomas to write *Under the Greenwood Tree*, which was published in 1872. It's a cheerful story of country folk, and incorporates real Dorset places into the plot, including the village school of Higher Bockhampton where Thomas went when he was eight. *This* book went down a storm with readers and reviewers.

Success at last! Thomas now wrote the romantic *A Pair of Blue Eyes*, which was published as a book in 1873. Then a different publisher asked Thomas to write a new novel to be serialized in its magazine. Not one to hang about, Thomas quickly produced *Far From the Madding Crowd*, which was first serialized and then published in book form in 1874. Briefly, the story goes a bit like this…

Far From The Madding Crowd was so successful that Thomas could finally give up architecture completely and concentrate on his writing. Over the next 20 years Thomas wrote another ten novels. He'd achieved his ambition, but he couldn't have realized just how famous and well-loved his books would become.

The Wessex Wizard

Thomas once wrote to one of his publishers:

Could you, whenever advertising my books, use the words 'Wessex Novels' at the head of the list?... I find that the name Wessex, which I was the first to use in fiction, is getting taken up everywhere...

Wessex was the old name for much of the south and southwest of England, and Thomas resurrected the name for his fiction. In 1918 Thomas met with the war poet Siegfried Sassoon, who christened him The Wessex Wizard.

Real places are instantly recognizable in Thomas's books, but he gave them different names. For example, Dorchester becomes Casterbridge in Hardy's novels, but it's the same place with the same buildings – for example, it's still possible to visit the King's Arms, where Michael Henchard has his council meeting near the beginning of *The Mayor of Casterbridge*.

It's grim down south

As well as being set in Wessex, many of Thomas's novels have another thing in common: they aren't very cheerful. In fact, they're tragic. They include lost love, murder, suicide, untimely death, rape, starvation, and more lost love. Remember Thomas's friend Horace from page 122? He had committed suicide in 1873, which had of course very much upset Thomas – maybe this was one of the things that made his books rather bleak.

For more than a century readers have wept buckets over the fate of poor, beautiful Tess in *Tess of the d'Urbervilles*. *The Mayor of Casterbridge* starts as it means to go on when the drunken central character *sells* his own wife and small child at a country fair, then spends the next 20 years bitterly regretting it … and of course much worse is still to come. But perhaps the most tragic of all (and the most shocking of all to its Victorian readers) is Thomas's last novel…

A cheat's guide to Jude the Obscure

Who's Jude? And why is he 'obscure'? At the beginning of the novel, Jude Fawley is a bright child from a poor family who dreams of going to college at Christminster (Thomas's name for Oxford) instead of remaining in obscurity and becoming an ordinary working man. As you might expect, Jude's dreams are never realized, but it gets an awful lot worse than that.

What's so tragic about it? Without going into the whole plot, it's a tale of unhappy marriages, shattered dreams and lots of death – even innocent little kids'.

Why was it such a shocker? Jude gets tricked into marrying someone he doesn't love. He later meets and falls in love with Sue, who is also already married. Jude and Sue live and have children together without being married. No one would think twice about a novel with this sort of plot now, but in 1895 it was shocking in the extreme.

What other people said about it: Jeannette Gilder wrote in the *New York World*: 'I am shocked, appalled by this story... It is almost the worst book I ever read... I thought that *Tess of the d'Urbervilles* was bad enough, but that is milk for babes compared to this... Aside from its immorality there is coarseness which is beyond belief.' The book sold well, but many readers hid their copies behind plain brown paper wrappers, and the Bishop of Wakefield burned his copy!

All the fuss provoked by *Jude the Obscure* was part of the reason why it was Thomas's last ever novel.

Today Thomas is best known for his famous novels, which have been made into films for TV and cinema, but his real passion was always poetry. Now that he had plenty of money from his books and no longer needed to earn a living from his writing, he returned to his first literary love, and for the rest of his long life he focused on poetry. He ended up with a whole shelf of poetry books as well as his novels.

Thomas and Emma

Having moved about a fair bit, in 1885 Thomas and Emma finally settled in a house Thomas had designed and had built, just on the outskirts of Dorchester.

Thomas may have been happy with Max Gate, but it wasn't very long before his marriage to Emma became very unhappy. Perhaps Thomas was thinking of himself and Emma when he wrote about Michael and Susan Henchard in *The Mayor of Casterbridge*:

> *That the man and woman were husband and wife, and the parents of the girl in arms there could be little doubt. No other than such relationship would have accounted for the atmosphere of stale familiarity which the trio carried along with them like a nimbus as they moved down the road.*

Emma became obsessed with the fact that Thomas wasn't as posh as she was (remember his dad was a stonemason and his mum had been a servant) and used to call Thomas a 'peasant'! The pair were also at odds about religion – Thomas had serious doubts it, while Emma was a conventional Christian.

Emma died suddenly in November 1912, and was buried in Stinsford churchyard, very near to the cottage where Thomas had been born. Despite the fact that he and Emma hadn't been happy for a long time, Thomas was overcome with guilt and grief. After all, they'd been married for 38 years.

A happier ending

In 1914 Thomas married Florence Dugdale, a children's book writer who had also been Thomas's secretary and housekeeper. There was quite a difference in age: he was 73 and she was 35! Despite that, and his strong feelings about his first wife, theirs does seem to have been a happy marriage.

In the last years of his life, Thomas continued to live at Max Gate in Dorchester with Florence, writing poetry and enjoying being a famous writer. He died at home on 11 January 1928, at the age of 88.

Thomas had said he wanted to be buried beside Emma in Dorset. But, rather gruesomely, only his heart was buried in Emma's grave. There's an even more gruesome story that Thomas's heart was left in the care of a maid, was stolen by a cat, and had to be replaced with a pig's heart! Thankfully, it's probably not true.

The rest of Thomas was honoured with a burial at Poets' corner in Westminster Abbey – just as Charles Dickens had been nearly 60 years earlier.

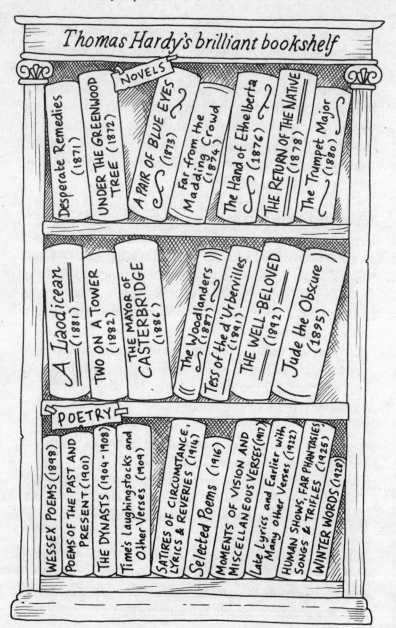

Thomas Hardy's brilliant bookshelf

NOVELS

Desperate Remedies (1871)
UNDER THE GREENWOOD TREE (1872)
A PAIR OF BLUE EYES (1873)
Far from the Madding Crowd (1874)
The Hand of Ethelberta (1876)
THE RETURN OF THE NATIVE (1878)
The Trumpet Major (1880)

A Laodicean (1881)
TWO ON A TOWER (1882)
THE MAYOR OF CASTERBRIDGE (1886)
The Woodlanders (1887)
Tess of the d'Urbervilles (1891)
THE WELL-BELOVED (1892)
Jude the Obscure (1895)

POETRY

WESSEX POEMS (1898)
POEMS OF THE PAST AND PRESENT (1901)
THE DYNASTS (1904-1908)
Time's Laughingstocks and Other Verses (1909)
SATIRES OF CIRCUMSTANCE, LYRICS & REVERIES (1914)
Selected Poems (1916)
MOMENTS OF VISION AND MISCELLANEOUS VERSES (1917)
Late Lyrics and Earlier with Many other Verses (1922)
HUMAN SHOWS, FAR PHANTASIES SONGS & TRIFLES (1925)
WINTER WORDS (1928)

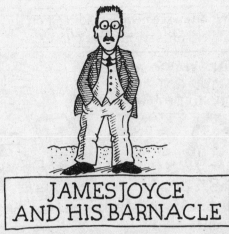

JAMES JOYCE AND HIS BARNACLE

Ask an adult why James Joyce is horribly famous and they'll nod wisely and say...

AH YES, ABSOLUTE GENIUS. HE WROTE ULYSSES.

Ask them whether or not they've read it and their answer will probably be...

UMM, WELL, NOT AS SUCH ... BITS OF IT, YES ... UMM...

James Joyce became horribly famous for writing a novel that was completely different from any other before it, but you don't often see people reading it on the bus. And as for the novel James wrote after *Ulysses*…

FINNEGANS WAKE – AH, YES. HAVEN'T YOU GOT ANY HOMEWORK TO DO? (WHIMPER!)

We'll get round to James's books a bit later. But first, let's meet the family…

From riches to rags

James was born in a Dublin suburb in 1882, the first surviving son of John and May Joyce. The family started out quite well-off…

MAY   JAMES   JOHN

But 12 house moves and 13 (count 'em) children later, things had got decidedly dodgy…

NINE OF JAMES'S TWELVE BROTHERS AND SISTERS SURVIVED BABYHOOD. – IT WASN'T UNCOMMON FOR CHILDREN TO DIE VERY YOUNG IN THOSE DAYS.

John Joyce's income had gradually dwindled to nothing over the years. He obviously wasn't very good at hanging on to money or jobs. On the other hand, he was very good at singing, drinking heavily and being loud in pubs – often all at the same time. Rather unwisely, John decided to mortgage his house to raise money to live on, and ended up with nearly as many mortgages as he had children (which is pretty impressive).

While the family fortunes were still looking good, James (or Sunny Jim as his parents called him) and his younger brother Stanislaus (known as Stannie) were sent to a posh boarding school for boys. They had to leave the school after just one year, when their parents couldn't afford the fees, but luckily they ended up with free places at another posh school.

Jim was a Catholic and both of his schools were run by Catholic priests called Jesuits. Punishment took the form of a beating with a leather thwacker called a 'pandybat', which Jim received at least once. Much later Jim would get his own back (well, sort of) by describing one particularly unfair and painful pandybatting in his first novel, *A Portrait of the Artist as a Young Man* (Jim was referring to himself as 'the Artist' in the title – the book is about his own early life). In the book, Jim also remembers the Jesuits' terrifying tales of damnation – here is a priest's description of hell from *A Portrait*:

> *Imagine some foul and putrid corpse that has lain rotting and decomposing in the grave, a jellylike mass of liquid corruption … devoured by the fire of burning brimstone and giving off dense choking fumes of nauseous loathsome decomposition. And then imagine this sickening stench, multiplied a millionfold … from the millions upon millions of fetid carcases massed together … a huge and rotting human fungus. Imagine all this and you will have some idea of the horror of the stench of hell.*

And you might be surprised to hear that hell gets a lot worse – the unbelievably foul stench is in fact the least of your worries. But despite being terrified for his immortal soul for much of the time, Jim did very well at school and won several prizes (which took the form of much-needed cash) for being generally very clever at more or less everything but especially English and languages. (As an adult, Jim could speak French, German and Italian fluently.) Generally, he was a bit of an all-round goody-goody.

Jim began to lose his Catholic faith in his early teens, and by the time he was about 16 he had more or less completely rejected it. Instead of thinking holy thoughts and working hard at school, Jim concentrated on his own writing. He was absolutely confident that he was going to be a writer – and a brilliant one at that.

Jim gets snooty

Jim had decided to be a bit of a slacker at school, but he didn't stop studying altogether. He read just about everything he could lay his hands on: he was a big fan of Thomas Hardy, and his absolute favourite writer was the Norwegian playwright Henrik Ibsen – both writers who were seen as a bit shocking.

In 1898, Jim went to University College, Dublin. He started his course as he meant to go on – by skipping classes and being rather arrogant. He continued with his writing, convinced that one day he would be recognized as the genius he was. And it wasn't long before he did indeed get something published...

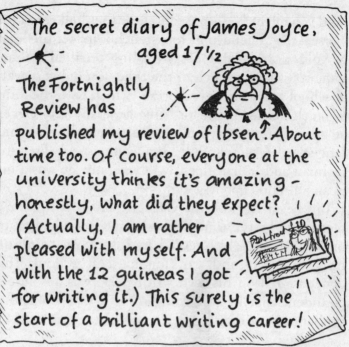

The secret diary of James Joyce,
aged 17½

The Fortnightly Review has published my review of Ibsen. About time too. Of course, everyone at the university thinks it's amazing – honestly, what did they expect? (Actually, I am rather pleased with myself. And with the 12 guineas I got for writing it.) This surely is the start of a brilliant writing career!

Encouraged by this, Jim went on to write plays and poetry of his own. None of James Joyce's published books has a dedication, but the first play he wrote did have a rather modest one:

```
To my own soul I dedicate the first
          true work of my life
```

Paris ... and some bad news

Jim finished his university course in 1902 and decided to study medicine ... in Paris. You might be wondering how someone from such a poor family could afford to spend his time studying abroad instead of being sent out to earn some money. John and May Joyce certainly were skint, but they both came from backgrounds where being cultured and educated were top priorities, plus they wholeheartedly agreed with Jim's high opinion of himself. So they were prepared to make sacrifices (usually in the form of more mortgages, or taking their possessions to a pawnbroker) in order to see that their children were as cultured and educated as possible. Which was lucky for Jim.

When he got to Paris, Jim didn't seem all that bothered about his medical course, and spent a lot of time reading, writing and hanging out in cafes with the new friends he made there. He tried to earn money to keep himself in food and obscure European literature by writing reviews for newspapers and giving private English lessons. He also borrowed money and cadged free meals as often as possible – he even sent begging letters home to his mum, who obliged him by pawning yet more possessions.

In fact, by this time poor May Joyce was very ill. On 10 April 1903 Jim received a telegram from his dad:

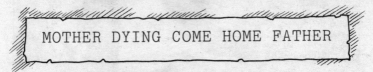

MOTHER DYING COME HOME FATHER

He had to borrow the money for his fare, but Jim went back to Dublin straight away.

May Joyce had cancer and, after several painful months, she died. John Joyce was grief-stricken, and so was the whole family. The household was left in a bit of a state, with the house itself in disrepair and not enough food to eat.

Rather unhelpfully, Jim began getting drunk a lot – perhaps to keep his dad company. He also earned some money writing reviews and, briefly, teaching at a private school. But he continued with his writing too: the year after his mother's death, in 1904, he began *Stephen Hero*, the novel about his childhood that later changed its title to *A Portrait of the Artist as a Young Man*.

Nora

Also in 1904, on 10 June, someone special sauntered cockily into Jim's life. She was a woman with one of the most memorable names ever associated with English literature…

Nora was a good-looking, straight-talking chambermaid from Galway City, who worked in Finn's Hotel in Dublin. Jim thought she was wonderful, and the pair fell in love. Their first date was on 16 June 1904. Many years later, Jim set all the action of his most famous novel, *Ulysses*, on that very date. Awww.

Nora and Jim were getting on so well that they decided to run away together (without getting married!) in

October 1904. (In fact they did end up getting married – but not for another 27 years.) The pair ended up in Trieste, which is now in Italy but used to be in Austria, where they were to stay for the next ten years (apart from one brief spell in Rome). Jim got a job teaching English in a language school called the Berlitz. He wasn't a conventional English teacher – his eccentric teaching methods later involved him sliding down the banisters during his private lessons!

In July 1905…

IT'S A BOY!

Nora and Jim named their son Giorgio after Jim's much-loved younger brother, George, who'd died three years before, at just 15 years old.

Long-suffering Stannie

In October the same year, Jim's brother Stannie came to join the family in Trieste, and was taken on as a second English teacher at the Berlitz school. He was to live either with Jim and Nora or very close by them for many years to come. Stannie was often called upon to pay Jim's debts and prevent the Joyce family from being evicted from various lodgings, which got on his nerves a bit. He blamed Jim's extravagant lifestyle for their grim financial situation: Jim and Nora were always eating in restaurants, and Jim was very fond of going out to bars, meeting up with friends and getting as drunk as possible.

A bothersome book and a bouncing baby

Alongside the excitement, fuss and bother of moving to a foreign country, getting a job and becoming a dad, Jim had also found time to write. By the end of 1905 he had written a book of poetry called *Chamber Music*, quite a bit more of *Stephen Hero*, and the first draft of his book of short stories about ordinary city folk, *Dubliners*. On 3 December 1905, Jim sent *Dubliners* to a London publisher called Grant Richards. It was the first step on a weary and very long road to publication…

James Joyce's secret Dubliners diary

CENSORED IN THE INTERESTS OF DECENCY!

February 1906

I have a contract from Grant Richards – he's definitely going to publish Dubliners. Well, I should think so too since it is rather brilliant. My first book! Hurrah!

May 1906
The printer says Dubliners is indecent! He's objecting to the word 'bloody' in my story 'Grace'. I've never heard such a load of **!!@?! The man's a *!*@%$!

November 1906
That coward Grant Richards isn't going to publish my stories after all. Indecent? I'll give him indecent - I'll *💀❀**!?@! the *@❀!! and then *!☻💀❀! That'll show him.
To be continued...

In 1907...

IT'S A GIRL!

Nora had her second child, called Lucia Anna, on 26 July. Another happy event took place the same year: *Chamber Music* (Jim's book of poetry) was published, which cheered him up a little bit after all the trouble he'd been having with *Dubliners*. But 1907 was a bad year for Jim's health: he got rheumatic fever and couldn't work at all for a while (which meant the family had to rely on Stannie for money), and he began to have problems with his eyes. Jim was plagued with eye trouble for the rest of his life, which meant periods of terrible pain during which he couldn't write. He had to have various operations and – ew, look away now if you're squeamish – even had leeches applied to his eyeballs!

Trouble in Dublin

Jim went back to Dublin three times between 1909 and 1912, twice to introduce his growing family to the other Joyces and Barnacles, and once to pursue his cinema scheme (see list of harebrained schemes on page 52). The visits were mostly happy, but the final one ended very badly indeed. Jim had found another publisher for *Dubliners*, a man named George Roberts of a Dublin publishing company, who kept promising publication dates that never happened.

James Joyce's Secret Dubliners Diary
September 1912, Dublin

GRRRRRR! I've been to George Roberts's office and had an ENORMOUS row with the lily-livered *!☺☼! I now discover that he has upset just about every author he's ever worked with. The man demanded changes, which I agreed to even though they were completely outrageous and unnecessary, then he said the book was anti-Irish and libellous and asked me - ME! - to pay him back the money he'd spent on getting the pages printed!!!!! I even offered to buy the proofs and get the **!!☼☺! book published myself, but that *!☼☠*!?! of a printer refused to hand them over! And today the final !☼#!*! straw - the proofs have been destroyed! *!@#☼☺ ☼!**!☺⚡☁*!!

Jim, Nora and the two nippers went back to Austria, never to return to Ireland again. Which is odd, really: Jim's writing is almost all set in his home city, and Dublin is lovingly recreated in the pages of his most famous book, *Ulysses*.

Harebrained schemes

Jim had various harebrained money-making schemes. Here are some of them:

• Becoming a singer – received voice training twice (1905 and 1908), both times abandoned.

• Importing Irish tweeds from Dublin to Trieste – which never quite came to anything.

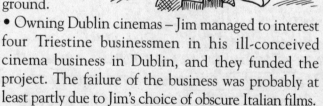

• Importing skyrockets to Trieste from Dublin – thankfully, Jim decided this would be too dangerous and the scheme never got off the ground.

• Owning Dublin cinemas – Jim managed to interest four Triestine businessmen in his ill-conceived cinema business in Dublin, and they funded the project. The failure of the business was probably at least partly due to Jim's choice of obscure Italian films.

• Producing plays in English in Zurich. Jim fell out with one of the main actors over money so badly that it resulted in a legal battle.

Literary lift-off

In 1913 Jim began to exchange letters with the rich American poet Ezra Pound (crazy name, crazy beard). Ezra introduced Jim to all sorts of useful people, including Harriet Weaver, who would turn out to be very useful indeed: Harriet serialized *A Portrait of the Artist as a Young Man* (the novel about Jim's childhood, which was now finished) in the magazine she edited in London. *Dubliners* was published in 1914 by Grant Richards – yes, the man who'd first agreed to publish it back in 1906! And Jim only had to wait another two years before *A Portrait* was published in book form: it came out in the USA in December 1916 and in England in 1917.

This was more like it! Encouraged by the praise he got from Ezra, Harriet and others – which he felt he richly deserved – and by the successful publication of his first novel, Jim worked as much as his eyesight would allow him (he had to have an eye operation in 1917). He began writing his next novel, *Ulysses*, in 1914 and by 1918 had completed the first three chapters – slow going, but Jim would labour over every word to make absolutely sure he'd got it right. He once proudly announced to a friend that he'd had a very productive day, having completed a single sentence…

What I am seeking is the perfect order of the words in the sentence. I think I have it.

In 1915, Jim started to receive money from various different sources, which allowed him to concentrate on his writing. It began with £75 from the Royal Literary Fund in England, continued with £50 from Harriet Weaver in 1916 as payment for serializing *A Portrait*, and got considerably better as time went on, including a massive £5,000 in 1917 from Jim's mystery benefactor (the mystery person later turned out to be none other than Harriet Weaver – whose considerable wealth Jim did his best to reduce as much as possible). Harriet and a selection of other rich people enabled Jim to keep writing without having to do too much work, though he still gave private English lessons.

It might have occurred to you by now that this period of European history was famous for something other than James Joyce's books and income…

The Daily Newspaper

28 July 1914

FIRST WORLD WAR DECLARED!

The War meant that Jim had to move to Zurich in Switzerland, where he stayed until the War was over, but he didn't seem particularly bothered about it apart from that. He was steadfastly uninterested in current affairs. He said much later:

What interests me is style, not politics.

In fact, Jim had spent most of his time during the War writing his most famous novel and first Very Difficult Book...

Ulysses

In March 1918, the New York literary magazine, the *Little Review*, began its serialization of *Ulysses* – Jim had only finished the first three chapters by this time. In case you haven't got time to nip off and quickly read it...

A cheat's guide to Ulysses

Yuley-who? Ulysses is the Roman name for Odysseus, the character from Greek mythology whose wanderings on his way home from the Trojan War are the subject of the ancient Greek epic poem by Homer, *The Odyssey*.

So it's about the Greek geezer? No, the main hero is a Jewish Dubliner called Leopold Bloom.

What's it got to do with Odysseus, then? Well, not a lot, apart from its structure. The adventures that happen to Odysseus – a fight with a one-eyed giant, a visit to the Underworld, etc – are reflected in the ordinary things that happen in one day to Bloom.

Why's it so famous? The style and subject was unlike any other novel before it, and it's most famous for being the first novel to make use of 'internal monologue', or 'stream of consciousness', where we follow a character's thoughts just as he or she thinks them. (So instead of saying 'Mary was thinking about chips', Jim would write something like 'gorgeous lovely chips, all hot and crisp and covered in salt and vinegar, mmmm can't wait for teatime'. Well, sort of.) Each sentence is packed with meanings – some of which you'd only be able to understand if you knew Jim's life in intimate detail.

What other people have said about it: 'I have read the first one hundred pages at least three times, and then, longing for a story, I never got further.' – Richard Bernstein, book critic of the *New York Times*, with whom many people would agree.

What Jim said about it: 'It is an epic of two races (Israelite–Irish) and at the same time the cycle of the human body as well as a little story (storiella) of a day (life)… It is also a sort of encyclopedia.'

Unfortunately, in 1920 instalments of *Ulysses* in the *Little Review* were stopped because the book was thought to be obscene – it's true that in the book someone farts and at one point two men go for a pee, rather shockingly. A trial took place in 1921 (by which time Jim had finished writing the book), when the court decided that *Ulysses* was indeed obscene and should be banned. The ban remained in force in the United States till 1933.

Back in October 1919 Jim, Nora and the children had returned to Trieste from Zurich, and moved in with Jim's sister Eileen, her husband and two children, and Stannie. So things were just a bit on the crowded side. Then, in July 1920, Joyce and Nora went to Paris to stay for one week – and ended up staying for 20 years!

Fame at last

Paris suited Jim, and he soon became friends with Sylvia Beach, the groovy owner of a groovy bookshop called Shakespeare & Co. Sylvia became another of Jim's devoted fans (he had a knack for finding these). She turned out to be a very useful one, too: just when it seemed that no one would ever publish *Ulysses*, Sylvia stepped in and the book was published by Shakespeare & Co on Jim's 40th birthday, 2 February 1922.

Jim now started to become famous. *Ulysses* proved to be controversial: some people agreed with Jim's opinion of himself – that he was a genius of the highest order – while others thought he was a fraud and his book was a load of old nonsense. But whether or not they were saying good things, people were certainly talking about him. Rumours began to circulate:

Some of them were at least partly true.

Work in progress

In 1923, Jim began his next Very Difficult Book. He called it *Finnegans Wake*, after an Irish ballad in which a hod-carrier is believed to be dead but revives at his funeral (or 'wake') when he smells whiskey. But, for some reason, Jim decided that the title should be a closely guarded secret, and he told only Nora. Everyone else just knew that Jim was writing a mysterious book they referred to as Work in Progress.

Jim was hard at work writing the new book for the next *17 years*. He continued to have terrible trouble with his eyes, and there were times when he actually went blind, so it was just as well that he was still being given money by Harriet Weaver. But when Harriet saw some of the writing she was funding, she became just slightly worried that Jim had gone completely nuts. Here's an example of why Harriet might have raised her eyebrows just a bit:

What clashes here of wills gen wonts, oystrygods gaggin fishygods! Brékkek Kékkek Kékkek Kékkek! Kóax Kóax Kóax! Ualu Ualu! Quaouauh!

Jim was achieving the impossible: he was writing an *even more* difficult book than *Ulysses*. He had invented his own language for the book, which consisted of Dublin dialect and lots of borrowings from other languages all jumbled up together. As you might imagine, most people found it almost impossible to read. Jim's long-time fans, Ezra Pound and Harriet Weaver, said...

I will have another go at it, but up to present I make nothing of it whatever.

It seems to me you are wasting your genius.

Stannie said he found it 'unspeakably wearisome'.

Jim still had the utmost confidence in his own abilities, and wasn't put off by all the criticism. He worked as hard as possible on the book, but he was having terrible problems with his eyes (by 1930, Jim had had *11* eye operations). He despaired of ever finishing it.

Eventually, Jim did complete *Finnegans Wake*. Now that he was famous, there was no problem with finding a publisher, and the London company Faber and Faber published the book in 1939. Some reviews were rather along these lines:

Yes, well. Umm … Mr Joyce is quite obviously a genius, and this … er … remarkable work is, um, proof of that. I think.

And, of course, a fair number of readers just thought Jim was completely barking mad. Nora, who never took much of an interest in Jim's writing, said:

> *Why don't you write sensible books that people can understand?*

...a question echoed by many readers.

A sad ending...

Two very sad things happened in the last ten years of Jim's life. First, his father, John Joyce, died in 1931 and Jim was devastated. Second, Jim's daughter Lucia was suffering from mental illness. Jim took her to see many different doctors in various parts of Europe, and for a time Lucia was treated by the famous psychoanalyst Carl Jung. But Lucia got worse and spent periods of time in mental asylums.

Time was running out for our hero. He and Nora returned to Zurich, where Jim died on 13 January 1941, shortly before his 59th birthday, after an operation on his stomach ulcer (maybe the drinking had something to do with that). Nora died ten years later.

...But a happy memorial

Jim is remembered as an eccentric genius, and his books are remembered and read as some of the most important of the twentieth century. He influenced many of the writers who followed him, but perhaps the best tribute to James Joyce is something that still happens every year on 16 June in the streets of Dublin: 'Bloomsday' is celebrated by fans of *Ulysses*, who recreate the activities and retrace the steps of Leopold Bloom, the book's hero.

James Joyce's brilliant bookshelf

Chamber Music (1907 - poems)

DUBLINERS (1914)

EXILE (1915 - PLAY)

A Portrait of the Artist as a Young Man (1916)

ULYSSES (1922)

POMES PENYEACH (1927 - poems)

Finnegans Wake (1939)

GEORGE ORWELL
AND HIS POWERFUL POLITICS

It's not many writers who get an adjective of their very own. George Orwell is one of them: if you look him up in a dictionary, you'll find something like:

Orwellian *adj*, characteristic of novelist George Orwell, particularly with reference to the type of state described in his novel *Nineteen Eighty-four*.

And he's added new words and phrases to our language ... including some that have ended up as TV programmes.

BIG BROTHER

ROOM 101

George Orwell is horribly famous. And he's also full of surprises...

A surprising start

The first surprise about George Orwell is that that isn't his name. He was born Eric Blair on 25 June 1903. And he wasn't born in Britain, as you might have expected, but in India. Eric and his family lived in a village called Motihari in Bengal, because Richard Blair (Eric's dad) worked for the Indian Civil Service.

Another surprise is that Eric's dad worked in the Opium Department. Opium is an illegal drug made from poppy seeds, so it's odd to think that a group of British officials used to be in charge of making it and distributing it around the world. In those days, of course, it wasn't illegal and opium made a lot of money for the government – mainly because it's a highly addictive drug.

By 1908, the family looked like this:

But a photo of the whole family was a rare thing: Ida, Marjorie and Eric went back to live in England in 1905 while Richard Blair stayed at his job in India. Mrs Blair and the little Blairs lived in the small, pretty town of Henley-on-Thames in Oxfordshire. Richard would only rarely get leave to come and see his family. (He came to England in 1907 – hence the arrival of Avril in 1908.) Richard only returned to live permanently with the rest of the family in 1912, once he'd retired.

St Cyprian's

In 1911 Ida Blair decided it was high time eight-year-old Eric was sent to school. With the help of Ida's brother, enough money was scraped together to send Eric to a fee-paying boarding school, St Cyprian's in Sussex. It's difficult to say whether he was happy there or not: more than 30 years later he bitterly criticized the school and its teachers for their cruelty, but none of his old school friends remembered it as being that bad, or that Eric was unhappy there. Of course, by modern standards it *was* that bad – beatings, Latin and ... *porridge* for breakfast.

We do know that Eric did brilliantly in his school work at St Cyprian's. He won various school prizes for his outstanding work and he was top of the class in Latin. And as well as being a bit of a swot, Eric also practised his writing. He later wrote:

From a very early age, perhaps the age of five or six, I knew that when I grew up I should be a writer.

At the beginning of the First World War, 11-year-old Eric had his first piece of writing published: in 1914 his patriotic poem about the War appeared in the local paper, urging people to enlist in the British Army and threatening to 'hurl troops at the Germans' and 'give them the hardest of knocks'. Gosh!

Part of the reason for sending Eric to St Cyprians was so that he might have the chance of winning a scholarship (i.e. he wouldn't have to pay school fees) to a *really* posh public school. In 1917 he did win a scholarship, to Eton – the poshest and most famous public school of them all.

Odd Eton

Eton was – and still is – full of odd traditions. For Eric and his schoolmates one of the most obvious was the bizarre uniform:

I FEEL LIKE A RIGHT TOP-HATTED TWIT!

Despite the top hat, Eric liked being at Eton...

The secret diary of Eric Blair, aged 14½

I worked like a dog at St Cyp's so that I could get here. Now I've arrived I'm going to have a lovely rest. I don't think I'll bother with any of the work at all – unless they set any that looks especially interesting (unlikely). Eton is a blessed relief: most of the chaps here seem like good eggs, I'm not going to bother with tiresome Latin any more, and I intend to spend my time lounging about reading (and perhaps writing, too). Huzzah!

One of his teachers later complained that Eric had done almost nothing in the four and a half years he was there. Sadly his school reports don't exist any more, but it's easy to imagine what they'd have looked like:

Eton school report for Eric Blair Michaelmas Half* 1919

Latin and Greek: *having been top in classics at his old school, Blair is now bottom of the class at Eton. What has happened? He doesn't seem to be doing any work at all! E*

Modern Languages: *Seems interested enough in class but his written work is either disappointing or never materializes. D*

Maths: *If Blair had actually produced any work I might be able to give him a report. E*

English: *Blair seems to have read an amazing amount of English literature, none of it on the curriculum and most of it quite unsuitable for a schoolboy. His marks for his work in this subject have been consistently appalling. E*

Instead of doing the work his teachers set for him, Eric spent his time reading books, getting involved with the Eton college magazine, playing sport and writing poetry – some of it for a friend on whom he had a bit of a crush, the wonderfully named Jacintha Buddicom.

* 'Half' was the Eton word for 'term' – another of the school's odd traditions.

Most students at Eton would expect to go on to Oxford or Cambridge, but Eric, being bottom of the class, failed to get a university place. Instead, he did something rather surprising for an English public schoolboy: he joined the Indian Imperial Police force.

Burmese days

Perhaps it wasn't such a strange thing for Eric to do: after all, his father had been a civil servant in India and his maternal grandmother still lived in Burma. In case you're wondering what on earth they were doing there… In the early 20th century, the British Empire was at its biggest. Britain ruled over Canada, a couple of bits of central America, large chunks of Africa, Australia and New Zealand, bits of Borneo and what's now Malaysia and Indonesia, and the whole of India and Burma – which is where Eric was headed.

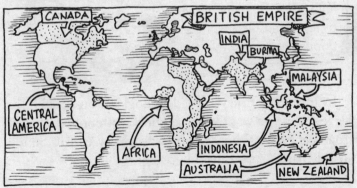

Swarms of British people went to live in the various parts of the Empire, either as administrators or to make huge sums of money at the native inhabitants' expense. Burma became part of the British Empire in the early 1900s. This meant that the British Army marched in, got rid of the monarchy, the nobles and the army, and started running the country, along with its very useful and plentiful supplies of money-making timber, rice and oil.

Eric trained in Burma and served there as an imperial policeman for nearly five years. It seems that he started out with a genuine enthusiasm for his job, but over time he couldn't help but see that the system he was defending was just a tad unfair, and he grew to hate it (he called it 'an unjustifiable tyranny' in one of his essays). In fact, he wrote a whole novel about it: *Burmese Days* has a British hero, Flory, who works in the timber industry and is disgusted by the British racists and the treatment of the Burmese. He tells his friend, a Burmese doctor:

> *My dear doctor ... how can you make out that we are in this country for any purpose except to steal? It's so simple. The official holds the Burman down while the businessman goes through his pockets.*

In July 1927 Eric returned to England on six months' leave. He never went back, sending a letter of resignation from his parents' house, which was now in the Suffolk seaside town of Southwold.

Down and out

While he'd been in Burma, Eric had hardly written anything. But he returned to England determined to try and become a writer. After a brief stay in Southwold, he rented a dingy London bedsit where he sat bashing away at his typewriter for a few months before leaving for Paris in 1928, thinking a change of scenery might be inspiring.

If you were a young, impoverished writer in the 1920s and 30s, Paris was definitely the place to be. While Eric was there, famous American writers Ernest Hemingway and F Scott Fitzgerald were both living there too. Only six years earlier *Ulysses* had been published by the Shakespeare & Co bookshop in Paris – Eric thought James Joyce was brilliant and kept an eye out for him. In fact, Eric thought Jim was so brilliant that he tried writing an 'experimental' novel like *Ulysses* himself, but he soon gave up. He had better success with a first draft of *Burmese Days* and with writing newspaper articles – the first of which was published in the Parisian *Monde* newspaper.

After a year or so living on very little money, writing and publishing a few articles, Eric embarked on another adventure – this time as a *plongeur*. Not a terribly thrilling adventure: *plongeur* means 'dishwasher'.

He spent nine months or so working in a flash Paris hotel and living among the poorest people in the city. He wanted to find out for himself what it was like to barely scrape a living and began to see the poor as victims of an unfair system – just like the Burmese. Eric  continued his social experiment when he returned to London in 1929: he made various trips to the very poorest parts of London, slept rough in Trafalgar Square, mixed with the homeless and stayed in the grottiest, cheapest lodging-houses in the city.

Based on his experiences, Eric finished a documentary-style book, which he called *A Scullion's Diary*, but he later changed its name to *Down and Out in Paris and London*.

The secret diary of Eric Blair, aged 26¾

All that grubbing around in foul, ghastly lodgings, eating revolting food and generally being horribly depressed hasn't been a waste of time: every privileged person should find out about the absolute beastliness of poverty. But I'm completely fed up with sending A Scullion's Diary round to publishers only to have it sent back by some snooty reader who's probably never read the damned thing anyway. So that's it! I've given it to Mabel and asked her to throw the whole shooting match away (but to keep the paperclips, there's no point in being wasteful, is there?). I'm still going to be a writer, of course – and not just a hack journalist either. I'll just have to think of something else.

Luckily, Eric's friend Mabel Fierz *didn't* throw the manuscript away: she kept it and took it to a literary agent she knew. Eventually, the publishing company Victor Gollancz accepted *Down and Out in Paris and London* and the book was published in 1933. Eric asked that the book be published under a pen name – he said it was because he wasn't proud of the book, which seems a bit odd: in that case why did he want to see it published at all? But whatever the reason, Eric became George (he'd never much liked the name Eric anyway) and Blair became Orwell, the name of a river in Suffolk. Since he didn't think much of being called Eric, let's call him George from now on.

Three books and two jobs

By the time *Down and Out* was published, George had finished his novel *Burmese Days*. But Victor Gollancz (the bloke who owned the publishing company) was nervous about what George had to say about the British Empire and he refused to publish it. In fact, the book ended up being published first in America, but things were off to a good start. George's next book, *A Clergyman's Daughter* was published in 1935. It also used some of his own experiences (such as sleeping rough in Trafalgar Square) and has a rather unlikely plot. George ended up hating it (he described it as 'tripe') and wouldn't allow it to be reprinted in his lifetime.

George was achieving his ambition of becoming a writer (even if he wasn't best pleased by some of his own work): by now he'd had three books published and was continuing to write articles and book reviews for newspapers and magazines. But the books weren't particularly successful and he still wasn't earning enough from his writing to live on. Having had a couple of stints as a private tutor in the summer of 1930 while he was staying with his family in Southwold, a couple of years later George became a schoolteacher in Hayes, Middlesex. There was only one problem: he absolutely hated it.

George had a much better time working part-time in a second-hand London bookshop as an assistant. He started the job in 1935, the year *A Clergyman's Daughter* and *Burmese Days* were published. In his spare time George was writing a new novel, *Keep the Aspidistra Flying* – the hero of which works in a second-hand bookshop and writes in his spare time but, unlike George, he has a thoroughly miserable time while he's doing it. Gollancz published *Keep the Aspidistra Flying* in 1936, but not before George had had another adventure...

Woeful Wigan

In 1936 Victor Gollancz asked George to do some research into social conditions in the North of England and write about it for the publisher's book club. Victor Gollancz was a company well-known for its left-wing politics. This meant being in favour of socialism – fairer distribution of wealth rather than a few fat cats having most of the money while ordinary working people struggle along being broke. George's opinions were along the same lines. He finished the manuscript he was working on, resigned from his job in the bookshop and set off for the North.

When George was writing, there was a big divide between rich and poor, and also between the North and the South of England. In the North were the coal mines and most of the country's manufacturing industry – and a lot of poverty. The South didn't have so much industry and no coal mines, but it was much more wealthy. Wigan, in the northwest of England, had very high unemployment – between a quarter and a third of the population. The book George wrote about his travels in Wigan and South Yorkshire, and conditions among the unemployed and coal-miners, became *The Road to Wigan Pier*, another work of non-fiction. In it George is very sympathetic towards the working people of the North of England, and conscious of the gap between his own privileged situation and theirs.

The book club liked the first half of the book but weren't very pleased with the second half, where George criticized English socialists: he said they were mostly middle-class types who didn't really know what they were talking about and put off decent working people by spouting nonsense. George wasn't a member of any political group or party – he liked to make up his own mind. When the book was published there was a foreword from the publisher arguing against some of the points made in the book!

George and Eileen

When he came back from his northern adventure, George decided to rent his Aunt Nellie's cottage in Wallington, Hertfordshire, rather than return to London. The cottage was called the 'Stores' because it had once been used as a general village shop – one of the ground-floor rooms had a shop counter in it. George cleared and planted the garden, bought a goat and some chickens, and the shop was re-opened barely six weeks after he'd moved in. The shop opening hours were morning only – George wrote in the afternoon. He made a start on *The Road to Wigan Pier* and continued his magazine and newspaper articles and reviews as well.

George had met Eileen O'Shaughnessy while he was in London the year before, and almost instantly decided he wanted to marry her. George had had various different girlfriends before, some of them quite serious, but Eileen, a pretty, dark-haired Londoner of Irish descent, was the only one he'd asked to marry him within a few weeks of meeting her. Eileen was witty and clever, and had an English degree from Oxford. When George met her she was studying for a Master's degree at University College, London.

In June 1936:

George and Eileen were married in the small church in Wallington.

Pain in Spain

The month after George and Eileen were married, political events unfolded in Spain that would have a dramatic effect on the couple (as well as on quite a few other people)…

The Socialist Standard
— 15 November 1936 —

SOCIALISTS UNITE!

Back in July, General Franco led a military revolt against the government in Spain. Franco is a fascist – he wants to make Spain a military country, restricting the rights of ordinary people. The Spanish people had voted for the old socialist government but a little thing like that didn't stop Franco from muscling in. The result has been the civil war that's still being fought.

But now socialists from all over the world have decided to come together and form the International Brigade to help the brave Spaniards fight fascistic Franco and send him packing for once and for all.

The Standard Says:
Are you a true socialist? (And if not, why are you reading this newspaper?) If the answer is yes, get yourself off to Spain immediately and help

George set off just before Christmas 1936, bound for Barcelona and the fighting.

The secret diary of George Orwell, aged 33½

January 1937

Arrived in Barcelona and joined one of the groups that's fighting Franco (POUM). The place is full of committed socialists with a real vision of a socialist future for Spain (once we get that !@※*!! Franco out of the way). People call one another 'comrade' but not in that ridiculous cringey way of those sandal-wearing English vegetarian twits back home, who call themselves socialists but plainly find it difficult mixing with the 'lower orders' and wouldn't know what a decent day's work <u>was</u>.

I'm to be trained at a barracks here for a while, then I'll be sent to the front at Alcubierre in north-eastern Spain, where the fighting is. I can hardly wait.

February 1937

Eileen's arrived! Aunt Nellie's looking after the shop in Wallington for us. Eileen's going to be working in the POUM offices in Barcelona while I'm at the front.

March 1937
Not an awful lot happens on the front line - not at all as I expected. Eileen came out to visit, though - we had our photo taken with the rest of the lads.

me→   Eileen

April 1937
Bored, bored, bored

May 1937
Nothing much to report. Still bored. Just having my usual morning cigarette in the trench. Hang on, what's that movement in the opposite trench, I . . . aaarrghhh ᵘᵘrrrk.

George woke up in hospital with a bullet wound in his throat – he was lucky to be alive. The doctor told him he'd never speak again, and at first his arm was paralysed, but happily he did manage to speak again (though his voice was a bit croaky), and the arm recovered.

But when George got out of hospital and back to Barcelona things had changed – there were fights between different socialist groups, and POUM was accused of secretly helping Franco. George and Eileen found themselves in danger of being shot or thrown in jail and were forced to run away to France. Despite the bad ending, George was very glad he'd been to Spain to at least try and fight against Franco. He wrote in a letter to a friend, 'I have seen wonderful things, and at last really believe in socialism.'

George and Eileen returned to London and then to Wallington, where George began writing an account of his time in Spain, published as *Homage to Catalonia*.

Time off sick

George had always had a weak chest, even as a child, which probably wasn't helped by the fact that he smoked like an especially rank factory chimney. But in 1938 his health took a very serious turn: George got tuberculosis.

The general opinion was that a warm climate would be good for George's condition, but he and Eileen didn't have much money. Luckily, though, a mystery donor (who turned out to be a rich author called L H Myers) provided them with enough funds to spend the winter somewhere warm. George and Eileen chose Morocco. Neither of them particularly liked it there, but the

climate must have done George some good. And he wrote a new novel in Morocco: *Coming Up for Air* was published the following year.

On his return to Wallington, George wrote three essays, later collected and published in a book called *Inside the Whale*, one of which was about our old friend, Charles Dickens. None of his books had done particularly well yet, but George was starting to get a reputation as an author.

More war and a farmyard
In 1939…

The Daily Newspaper

IT'S WAR!

Britain has declared war on Germany. Prime Minister Chamberlain said today that he was

George wanted to fight against the German Nazis, but he was declared unfit and had to make do with joining the Local Defence Force (also known as the Home Guard) instead. Eileen found a job in London while George stayed in Wallington. It was a miserable time and George didn't feel much like writing. And as if the war with Germany wasn't depressing enough, the news from Spain was that Franco (helped by the fascist governments in Germany and Italy) had beaten the socialists and now ruled the country as a dastardly dictator.

In order to earn money George wrote for newspapers and magazines, which he found a bit tiresome. He took a job as theatre critic for the magazine *Time and Tide*, and moved to London with Eileen. In 1941 George left the magazine and joined the BBC's Eastern Service as a broadcaster of a programme for India and the Far East. He didn't much like the work, wondering if anyone was actually listening to the programme, but he stayed there for two years until he was offered a job that suited him a bit better: literary editor of the *Tribune*, a left-wing magazine.

Towards the end of the War, George began writing his short novel, *Animal Farm*. It's a fable, simply told, of a group of farm animals...

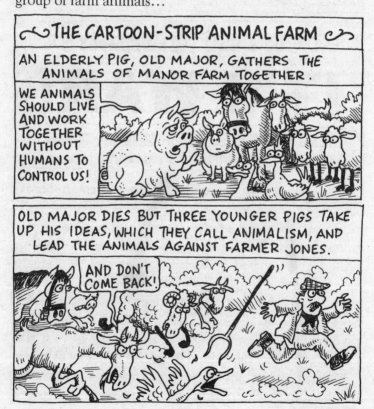

ANIMAL FARM, AS IT'S NOW CALLED, PROSPERS.

ANIMAL FARM.

MANOR FARM.

BUT ONE OF THE PIGS, NAPOLEON, USES HIS SECRETLY TRAINED TEAM OF ATTACK DOGS TO CHASE AWAY HIS RIVAL, AND MAKES SOME CHANGES.

FROM NOW ON, NO MORE MEETINGS. US PIGS MAKE ALL THE DECISIONS. AND NO ARGUMENTS!

NAPOLEON USES HIS DOGS TO KILL ANYONE WHO OPPOSES HIM OR WHOM HE SUSPECTS OF SUPPORTING HIS RIVAL.

NAPOLEON'S ALWAYS RIGHT - ANYONE WHO DISAGREES GETS IT!

THE ANIMALS ARE OVERWORKED AND HUNGRY.

NAPOLEON'S A GREAT LEADER. I HOPE NO ONE'S SAYING ANY DIFFERENT?

THE GHASTLY NAPOLEON STARTS BEHAVING MORE AND MORE LIKE A HUMAN.

HIC!

NAPOLEON DESCRIBES TO FARMER PILKINGTON HIS PLAN FOR UNITING THE LEADING PIGS AND HUMANS AGAINST THE WORKING ANIMALS AND HUMANS.

FROM OUTSIDE, THE OTHER ANIMALS CAN'T TELL WHICH ARE THE PIGS AND WHICH ARE THE HUMANS.

The story parallels the history of the Russian Revolution of 1917, which got rid of the monarchy (Farmer Jones's real-life counterpart), and the founding of the communist Soviet Union. The idea of communism is that all property is owned collectively by everyone, with people contributing as much as they can to the community and receiving from it as much as they need. But things didn't quite work out that way: from the late 1920s Josef Stalin got rid of his political rival and became the single leader of the Soviet Union (he was Napoleon the pig's real-life counterpart). No one could argue with Stalin – anyone who did was killed or sent to a prison camp. It was now a totalitarian state (which means everything is controlled by a single authority and no opposition allowed). George wrote in an essay:

> *Every line of serious work that I have written since 1936 has been written, directly or indirectly, against totalitarianism and for democratic socialism, as I understand it.*

His two most famous books, *Animal Farm* and *Nineteen Eighty-four*, are perfect examples.

Gollancz refused to publish *Animal Farm* because it was a criticism of the Soviet Union, which many left-wingers wanted to believe had been a success. (They were the sort of left-wingers who really annoyed George.) It took George 18 months to find a different publisher, but the book was eventually published in 1945. Then something really surprising happened: *Animal Farm* was an enormous success.

Fame and some tragic news

In 1944 George and Eileen made room in their north London flat for a new arrival: they adopted a baby son, Richard. George had always liked children and was very happy with this new arrangement.

He carried on working at the *Tribune* until, in 1945, George visited Austria, Germany and France as a war correspondent. While he was away a letter from Eileen told him that she was to have an operation: some tumours had been found and she needed to have them removed. It was a serious operation, but no one expected what happened next: Eileen never woke up from the anaesthetic.

George went back to London, looked after Richard and made arrangements for Eileen's funeral. Then he decided to leave Richard with some close friends while he returned to Europe for a while to continue with his job.

Suddenly, George was in circumstances he could never have predicted: his wife was dead, he had a young son, and he was a famous writer (and quite a rich one, too). Eileen never saw the huge success that George now found with *Animal Farm*.

George kept up with various different kinds of writing for magazines and newspapers despite his failing health (he had tuberculosis again). He also embarked on a series of marriage proposals to various different women, some of whom he barely knew (one, Anne Popham, he'd met on the stairs to his flat). And he started a new novel.

Nineteen forty-eight

Early in 1946 George had some more bad news: his older sister Marjorie died unexpectedly of kidney failure. He travelled up to Nottingham for her funeral, then visited his wife's grave in Newcastle. Then, in May 1946, George took off to the remote Hebridean island of Jura, where he could write in peace. Over the next couple of years, dividing his time between Jura and London, George wrote his most famous book, *Nineteen Eighty-four*.

A cheat's guide to Nineteen Eighty-four

Why 1984? George simply turned around the last two digits of the year he finished the novel to make a title for his terrifying vision of the future (which is in some ways a distorted version of 1948).

What's it all about? The novel is about the worst of all possible worlds: England is now known as Airstrip One, part of the state of Oceania, which is constantly at war with one of two other superstates. Telescreens continuously monitor everyone ('Big Brother is watching you!'),

there is constant propaganda and no one is allowed to argue with what the state says. Language is being changed in order to control the way people think – a 'Newspeak' dictionary compiler says: '… we shall make thoughtcrime literally impossible, because there will not be words in which to express it.' The hero, Winston Smith, has a job changing old issues of newspapers so that they don't contradict whatever is the current party line. Winston begins to hate the system and has a love affair with a woman who is similarly anti-government. As you might expect, they don't live happily ever after. A particularly terrifying moment comes when Winston has to confront his greatest fear in Room 101.

What other people have said about it: 'Newspeak, Doublethink, Big Brother, the Thought Police – George Orwell's world-famous novel coined new and potent words of warning for us all. Alive with Swiftian wit and passion, it is one of the most brilliant satires on totalitarianism and the power-hungry ever written' – Peter Quennell, critic.

What George said about it: 'I am not pleased with it, but I think it is a good idea.'

Marriages and deaths

George's tuberculosis was getting worse and he'd had to spend long periods in hospital at different times. His sister Avril was doing most of the caring for George's son Richard. But on 13 October 1949 George did another surprising thing: after an especially nasty bout of illness, he somehow found the strength to get married, to a young woman called Sonia Brownell. The wedding took place in an unusual location…

…room 65 at University College Hospital in London – George wasn't well enough to get out of bed.

On 21 January 1950 George died, aged only 46. Richard went to live in Scotland with Avril and her husband (she married the year after George died). George left them an impressive shelf of books to remember him by:

George Orwell's brilliant bookshelf

DOWN AND OUT IN PARIS AND LONDON (1933)

BURMESE DAYS (1934)

A Clergyman's Daughter (1935)

KEEP THE ASPIDISTRA FLYING (1936)

The Road to WIGAN PIER (1937)

HOMAGE TO CATALONIA (1938)

Coming up for Air (1939)

INSIDE THE WHALE (collection of essays 1940)

ANIMAL FARM (1945)

Critical Essays (1946)

NINETEEN EIGHTY-FOUR (1949)

SHOOTING AN ELEPHANT (collection of essays 1950)

THE FINAL CHAPTER

George Orwell said in his essay 'Why I Write':

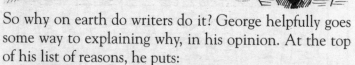

> *All writers are vain, selfish, and lazy, and at the very bottom of their motives there lies a mystery. Writing a book is a horrible, exhausting struggle, like a long bout of some painful illness.*

So why on earth do writers do it? George helpfully goes some way to explaining why, in his opinion. At the top of his list of reasons, he puts:

> *Sheer egoism. Desire to seem clever, to be talked about, to be remembered after death, to get your own back on the grown-ups who snubbed you in childhood, etc.*

Although George doesn't make writers sound like very nice people, these do sound like pretty good reasons, especially the last one. So if you want to get your revenge on the horrible old lady next door, or your very worst teacher, what's the best way to go about it?

There's no easy answer. All the different writers in this book have penned stories with completely different subjects and they've gone about it in all sorts of ways. William Shakespeare wrote plays and poems about historical characters, made-up kings and queens, jealous generals and fairies in an English forest. Jane Austen limited herself to writing novels about upper-class English people getting married – she would never have written about a group of Scottish witches.

James Joyce took enormous trouble to invent an entirely new way of writing, one that makes the inside of his characters' heads just as important as what's going on outside. And, as we've just found out, George Orwell felt the only really important thing to write about was politics – whether as fiction or non-fiction.

But, in a way, every writer's subject matter is the same. They all write about the things that have fascinated people since before writing was invented: love, hate, death, power, ambition, jealousy … pride and prejudice.

Maybe our famous writers have some tips for writing a bestseller.

The bestselling stories in this book have stood the test of time because they express the things that interest people most in a unique way. So, if you want to become a famous writer, you'll just have to find your own special way of doing it.